# Learning Cypher

Write powerful and efficient queries for Neo4j with
Cypher, its official query language

**Onofrio Panzarino**

BIRMINGHAM - MUMBAI

# Learning Cypher

Copyright © 2014 Packt Publishing

First published: May 2014

Production Reference: 1070514

Published by Packt Publishing Ltd.
Livery Place
35 Livery Street
Birmingham B3 2PB, UK.

ISBN 978-1-78328-775-8

www.packtpub.com

Cover Image by Jaroslaw Blaminsky (milak6@wp.pl)

# Credits

**Author**
Onofrio Panzarino

**Reviewers**
Riccardo Mancinelli

Rohit Mukherjee

Timmy Storms

Craig Taverner

**Commissioning Editor**
Antony Lowe

**Acquisition Editor**
Owen Roberts

**Content Development Editor**
Priyanka S

**Technical Editors**
Taabish Khan

Nikhil Potdukhe

Akash Rajiv Sharma

**Copy Editors**
Mradula Hegde

Gladson Monteiro

**Project Coordinator**
Harshal Ved

**Proofreader**
Ameesha Green

**Indexer**
Mariammal Chettiyar

**Graphics**
Yuvraj Mannari

Abhinash Sahu

**Production Coordinator**
Aparna Bhagat

**Cover Work**
Aparna Bhagat

# About the Author

**Onofrio Panzarino** is a programmer with 15 years experience working with various languages (mostly with Java), platforms, and technologies. Before obtaining his Master of Science degree in Electronics Engineering, he worked as a digital signal processor programmer. Around the same time, he started working as a C++ developer for embedded systems and PCs. Currently, he is working with Android, ASP.NET or C#, and JavaScript for Wolters Kluwer Italia. During these years, he gained a lot of experience with graph databases, particularly with Neo4j.

Onofrio resides in Ancona, Italy. His Twitter handle is (@onof80). He is a speaker in the local Java user group and also a technical writer, mostly for Scala and NoSQL. In his spare time, he loves playing the piano with his family and programming with functional languages.

First and foremost, I would like to thank my wife, Claudia, and my son, Federico, who patiently supported me at all times.

Special thanks to the team at Packt Publishing. It has been a great experience to work with all of you. The work of all the reviewers was invaluable as well.

I would also like to thank all my friends who read my drafts and gave me useful suggestions.

# About the Reviewers

**Riccardo Mancinelli** has acquired a degree in Electronics Engineering. He has more than nine years of experience in IT, specializing in frontend and backend software development. He currently works as an IT architect consultant and a senior Java developer.

He loves any tool and programming language that will help him achieve his goal easily and quickly. Besides programming, his favorite hobby is reading.

**Rohit Mukherjee** is a student of computer engineering at the National University of Singapore (NUS). He is passionate about software engineering and new technologies. He is currently based in Zurich, Switzerland, on a student exchange program at ETH, Zurich.

Rohit has worked for Ernst and Young in Kolkata, Bank of America Merrill Lynch in Singapore, and Klinify in Singapore.

He was a technical reviewer for *Google Apps Script for Beginners*, *Serge Gabet*, *Packt Publishing*.

I would like to thank my parents for their support.

**Timmy Storms** started working as a Java consultant after he completed his Bachelor's degree in Information Technology. He acquired SCJP, SCWCD, and SCBCD certifications to boost his overall Java knowledge. Over the years, he has worked in several industries, such as banking, and health care as well as for the government, where he gained a broad overview of the Java landscape. In the initial years of his career, he worked mostly as a frontend developer, but later on shifted his focus to backend technology.

He discovered the wonderful world of graph databases, and especially Neo4j, in late 2012. After he developed a social platform, he quickly saw the benefits of Neo4j and its query language Cypher. Being an early adopter of modules such as Spring Data Neo4j and cypher-dsl, he has made some contributions to the source code as well. He tries to help out as much as he can on topics pertaining to Neo4j and Cypher tags on www.stackoverflow.com. *Learning Cypher* is the first book that he has reviewed, and he doesn't expect it to be his last one.

**Craig Taverner** is an open source software developer, technology enthusiast, and entrepreneur working on many projects, especially those that involve Ruby, GIS, and Neo4j. He is the CTO and co-founder of AmanziTel AB, where he helps build really cool telecom statistics platforms.

Having a background in pure science, Craig has spent the last two decades working mostly in the mobile telecom field, where he has applied his analytical skills to help large international operators solve their complex data analysis problems. During this time, he has also contributed to several open source projects, most notably Neo4j Spatial, as well as presented at many conferences, such as FOSS4G 2010 and 2011 and GraphConnect 2012 and 2013. In addition, he has reviewed several technical books, including *Domain Specific Languages, Martin Fowler, Addison-Wesley Professional*; *Linked Data, David Wood and Marsha Zaidman, Manning Publications*; and *Neo4j in Action, Jonas Partner, Aleksa Vukotic, and Nicki Watt, Manning Publications*.

# www.PacktPub.com

## Support files, eBooks, discount offers, and more

You might want to visit www.PacktPub.com for support files and downloads related to your book.

Did you know that Packt offers eBook versions of every book published, with PDF and ePub files available? You can upgrade to the eBook version at www.PacktPub.com and as a print book customer, you are entitled to a discount on the eBook copy. Get in touch with us at service@packtpub.com for more details.

At www.PacktPub.com, you can also read a collection of free technical articles, sign up for a range of free newsletters and receive exclusive discounts and offers on Packt books and eBooks.

http://PacktLib.PacktPub.com

Do you need instant solutions to your IT questions? PacktLib is Packt's online digital book library. Here, you can access, read and search across Packt's entire library of books.

## Why subscribe?

- Fully searchable across every book published by Packt
- Copy and paste, print and bookmark content
- On demand and accessible via web browser

## Free access for Packt account holders

If you have an account with Packt at www.PacktPub.com, you can use this to access PacktLib today and view nine entirely free books. Simply use your login credentials for immediate access.

# Table of Contents

# Preface

Among the NoSQL databases, **Neo4j** is generating a lot of interest due to the following set of features: performance and scalability, robustness, its very natural and expressive graph model, and ACID transactions with rollbacks.

Neo4j is a graph database. Its model is simple and based on nodes and relationships. The model is described as follows:

- Each node can have a number of relationships with other nodes
- Each relationship goes from one node either to another node or the same node; therefore, it has a direction and involves either only two nodes or only one
- Both nodes and relationships can have properties, and each property has a name and a value

Before Neo4j introduced Cypher as a preferred query, utilizing Neo4j in a real-world project was difficult compared to a traditional relational database. In particular, querying the database was a nightmare, and executing a complex query required the user to write an object, thereby performing a graph traversal. Roughly speaking, a traversal is an operation that specifies how to traverse a graph and what to do with the nodes and relationships found during the visit. Though it is very powerful, it works in a very procedural way (through callbacks), so its readability is poor and any change to the query means modifying the code and building it.

Cypher, instead, provides a declarative syntax, which is readable and powerful, and a rich set of graph patterns that can be recognized in the graph. Thus, with Cypher, you can write (and read) queries much more easily and be productive from the beginning. This book will guide you through learning this language from the ground up, and each topic will be explained with a real-world example.

# What this book covers

*Chapter 1, Querying Neo4j Effectively with Pattern Matching*, describes the basic clauses and patterns to perform read-only queries with Cypher.

*Chapter 2, Filter, Aggregate, and Combine Results*, describes clauses and tips that can be used with patterns to elaborate results that come from pattern matching.

*Chapter 3, Manipulating the Database*, covers the write clauses, which are needed to modify a graph.

*Chapter 4, Improving Performance*, talks about tools and practices to improve performances of queries.

*Chapter 5, Migrating from SQL*, explains how to migrate a database to Neo4j from the ground up through an example.

*Appendix, Operators and Functions*, describes Cypher operators and functions in detail.

# What you need for this book

First and foremost, you need Neo4j. The community edition is free and open source. It can be downloaded from `http://www.neo4j.org/download`.

In the initial chapters, the examples are created using embedded Neo4j. To run the Java code, you need any Java IDE and Maven.

If you read this book on a tablet with an Internet connection, another way to run the Cypher code is using the Neo4j Console (`http://console.neo4j.org/`); it allows you to run Cypher queries directly in your browser and lets you to see the results immediately.

# Who this book is for

If you are a developer who wants to learn Cypher to interact with Neo4j and find out the capabilities of this language, this book is for you.

The first chapter assumes that you are a little familiar with the Java syntax; anyway, you don't require Java to understand Cypher examples that can be launched in the Neo4j console.

The last chapter on migration from SQL assumes you know SQL and the relational model.

# Conventions

In this book, you will find a number of styles of text that distinguish between different kinds of information. Here are some examples of these styles and an explanation of their meaning.

Code words in text, database table names, folder names, filenames, file extensions, pathnames, dummy URLs, user input, and Twitter handles are shown as follows: "We can assign starting points to variables in the query using the START keyword."

A block of code is set as follows:

```
START a=node(2), b=node(3)
RETURN allShortestPaths((a)-[*]-(b)) AS path
```

When we wish to draw your attention to a particular part of a code block, the relevant lines or items are set in bold:

```
MATCH (n:Employee {surname: {inputSurname}})
RETURN n
```

Any command-line input or output is written as follows:

```
# bin\Neo4jInstaller.bat install
```

**New terms** and **important words** are shown in bold. Words that you see on the screen, in menus or dialog boxes for example, appear in the text like this: "In the next page of the wizard, name the project, set a valid project location, and then click on **Finish**."

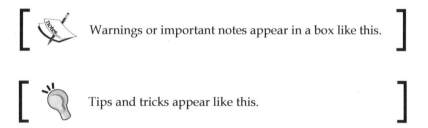

Warnings or important notes appear in a box like this.

Tips and tricks appear like this.

# Reader feedback

Feedback from our readers is always welcome. Let us know what you think about this book—what you liked or may have disliked. Reader feedback is important for us to develop titles that you really get the most out of.

To send us general feedback, simply send an e-mail to feedback@packtpub.com, and mention the book title via the subject of your message.

If there is a topic that you have expertise in and you are interested in either writing or contributing to a book, see our author guide on www.packtpub.com/authors.

# Customer support

Now that you are the proud owner of a Packt book, we have a number of things to help you to get the most from your purchase.

## Downloading the example code

You can download the example code files for all Packt books you have purchased from your account at http://www.packtpub.com. If you purchased this book elsewhere, you can visit http://www.packtpub.com/support and register to have the files e-mailed directly to you.

## Errata

Although we have taken every care to ensure the accuracy of our content, mistakes do happen. If you find a mistake in one of our books—maybe a mistake in the text or the code—we would be grateful if you would report this to us. By doing so, you can save other readers from frustration and help us improve subsequent versions of this book. If you find any errata, please report them by visiting http://www.packtpub.com/submit-errata, selecting your book, clicking on the **errata submission form** link, and entering the details of your errata. Once your errata are verified, your submission will be accepted and the errata will be uploaded on our website, or added to any list of existing errata, under the Errata section of that title. Any existing errata can be viewed by selecting your title from http://www.packtpub.com/support.

# Piracy

Piracy of copyright material on the Internet is an ongoing problem across all media. At Packt, we take the protection of our copyright and licenses very seriously. If you come across any illegal copies of our works, in any form, on the Internet, please provide us with the location address or website name immediately so that we can pursue a remedy.

Please contact us at `copyright@packtpub.com` with a link to the suspected pirated material.

We appreciate your help in protecting our authors, and our ability to bring you valuable content.

# Questions

You can contact us at `questions@packtpub.com` if you are having a problem with any aspect of the book, and we will do our best to address it.

# 1
# Querying Neo4j Effectively with Pattern Matching

Querying a graph database using the Java API can be very tedious; you would need to visit the whole graph and skip nodes that don't match what you are searching for. Any changes to the query will result in rethinking the code, changing it, and building it all over again. Why? The reason is that we are using an imperative language to do pattern matching, and traditional imperative languages don't work well in this task. **Cypher** is the declarative query language used to query a Neo4j database. Declarative means that it focuses on the aspects of the result rather than on methods or ways to get the result so that it is human-readable and expressive.

In this chapter, we will cover the following topics:

- Setting up a Neo4j database
- Querying the database in a simpler way than using the Java API

## Setting up a new Neo4j database

If you already have experience in creating a Neo4j database, you can skip this and jump to the next section.

Neo4j is a graph database, which means that it does not use tables and rows to represent data logically; instead, it uses **nodes** and **relationships**. Both nodes and relationships can have a number of properties. While relationships must have one direction and one type, nodes can have a number of labels. For example, the following diagram shows three nodes and their relationships, where every node has a label (language or graph database), while relationships have a type (**QUERY_LANGUAGE_OF** and **WRITTEN_IN**).

The properties used in the graph shown in the following diagram are name, type, and from. Note that every relation must have exactly one type and one direction, whereas labels for nodes are optional and can be multiple.

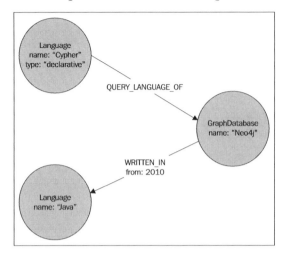

# Neo4j running modes

Neo4j can be run in two modes:

- An embedded database in a Java application
- A standalone server via REST

In any case, this choice does not affect the way you query and work with the database. It's an architectural choice driven by the nature of the application (whether a standalone server or a client server), performance, monitoring, and safety of data.

# Neo4j Server

Neo4j Server is the best choice for interoperability, safety, and monitoring. In fact, the REST interface allows all modern platforms and programming languages to interoperate with it. Also, being a standalone application, it is safer than the embedded configuration (a potential crash in the client wouldn't affect the server), and it is easier to monitor. If we choose to use this mode, our application will act as a client of the Neo4j server.

To start Neo4j Server on Windows, download the package from the official website (http://www.neo4j.org/download/windows), install it, and launch it from the command line using the following command:

```
C:\Neo4jHome\bin\Neo4j.bat
```

You can also use the frontend, which is bundled with the Neo4j package, as shown in the following screenshot:

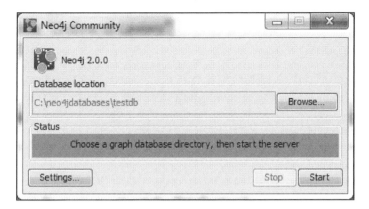

To start the server on Linux, you can either install the package using the Debian package management system, or you can download the appropriate package from the official website (http://www.neo4j.org/download) and unpack it with the following command:

```
# tar -cf  <package>
```

After this, you can go to the new directory and run the following command:

```
# ./bin/neo4j console
```

Anyway, when we deploy the application, we will install the server as a Windows service or as a daemon on Linux. This can be done easily using the Neo4j installer tool.

On the Windows command launch interface, use the following command:

```
# bin\Neo4jInstaller.bat install
```

When installing it from the Linux console, use the following command:

```
# neo4j-installer install
```

To connect to Neo4j Server, you have to use the REST API so that you can use any REST library of any programming language to access the database. Though any programming language that can send HTTP requests can be used, you can also use online libraries written in many languages and platforms that wrap REST calls, for example, Python, .NET, PHP, Ruby, Node.js, and others.

# An embedded database

An embedded Neo4j database is the best choice for performance. It runs in the same process of the client application that hosts it and stores data in the given path. Thus, an embedded database must be created programmatically. We choose an embedded database for the following reasons:

- When we use Java as the programming language for our project
- When our application is standalone

For testing purposes, all Java code examples provided with this book are made using an embedded database.

## Preparing the development environment

The fastest way to prepare the IDE for Neo4j is using **Maven**. Maven is a dependency management as well as an automated building tool. In the following procedure, we will use **NetBeans 7.4**, but it works in a very similar way with the other IDEs (for Eclipse, you will need the **m2eclipse** plugin). The procedure is described as follows:

1. Create a new Maven project as shown in the following screenshot:

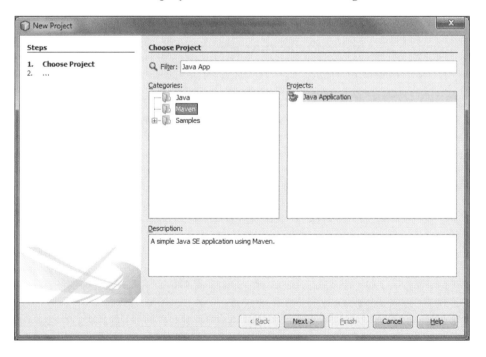

2. In the next page of the wizard, name the project, set a valid project location, and then click on **Finish**.

3. After NetBeans has created the project, expand **Project Files** in the project tree and open the `pom.xml` file. In the `<dependencies>` tag, insert the following XML code:

```
<dependencies>
  <dependency>
   <groupId>org.neo4j</groupId>
   <artifactId>neo4j</artifactId>
   <version>2.0.1</version>
  </dependency>
</dependencies>

<repositories>
  <repository>
    <id>neo4j</id>
<url>http://m2.neo4j.org/content/repositories/releases/</url>
    <releases>
      <enabled>true</enabled>
    </releases>
  </repository>
</repositories>
```

This code informs Maven about the dependency we are using on our project, that is, Neo4j. The version we have used here is 2.0.1. Of course, you can specify the latest available version.

If you are going to use Java 7, and the following section is not present in the file, then you'll need to add the following code to instruct Maven to compile Java 7:

```
<build>
  <plugins>
   <plugin>
     <groupId>org.apache.maven.plugins</groupId>
     <artifactId>maven-compiler-plugin</artifactId>
     <version>3.1</version>
     <configuration>
       <source>1.7</source>
       <target>1.7</target>
     </configuration>
   </plugin>
  </plugins>
</build>
```

Once saved, the Maven file resolves the dependency, downloads the JAR files needed, and updates the Java build path. Now, the project is ready to use Neo4j and Cypher.

## Creating an embedded database

Creating an embedded database is straightforward. First of all, to create a database, we need a `GraphDatabaseFactory` class, which can be done with the following code:

```
GraphDatabaseFactory graphDbFactory = new GraphDatabaseFactory();
```

Then, we can invoke the `newEmbeddedDatabase` method with the following code:

```
GraphDatabaseService graphDb = graphDbFactory
        .newEmbeddedDatabase("data/dbName");
```

Now, with the `GraphDatabaseService` class, we can fully interact with the database, create nodes, create relationships, and set properties and indexes.

## Configuration

Neo4j allows you to pass a set of configuration options for performance tuning, caching, logging, file system usage, and other low-level behaviors. The following code sets the size of the memory allocated for mapping the node store to 20 MB:

```
import org.neo4j.graphdb.factory.GraphDatabaseSettings;
// ...
GraphDatabaseService db = graphDbFactory
                .newEmbeddedDatabaseBuilder(DB_PATH)
                .setConfig(GraphDatabaseSettings
                    .nodestore_mapped_memory_size, "20M")
                .newGraphDatabase();
```

You will find all the available configuration settings in the `GraphDatabaseSettings` class (they are all static final members).

Note that the same result can be achieved using the `properties` file. Clearly, reading the configuration settings from a `properties` file comes in handy when the application is deployed because any modification to the configuration won't require a new build. To replace the preceding code, create a file and name it, for example, `neo4j.properties`. Open it with a text editor and write the following code in it:

```
neostore.nodestore.db.mapped_memory=20M
```

Then, create the database service with the following code:

```
GraphDatabaseService db = graphDbFactory
                .newEmbeddedDatabaseBuilder(DB_PATH)
                .loadPropertiesFromFile("neo4j.properties")
                .newGraphDatabase();
```

# HR management tool – an example

For the first example in this book, I chose an enterprise application, such as **human resource (HR)** management, because I think Neo4j is a great persistence tool for enterprise applications. In fact, they are famous for having very complex schemas with a lot of relationships and entities and requirements that often change during the life of the software; therefore, the queries are also complicated and prone to change frequently.

> **Downloading the example code**
>
> You can download the example code files for all Packt books you have purchased from your account at http://www.packtpub.com. If you purchased this book elsewhere, you can visit http://www.packtpub.com/support and register to have the files e-mailed directly to you.

In our human resources tool, we have two kinds of nodes: employees and cost centers. So, we can define the two labels with the following code:

```
public enum HrLabels implements Label {
    Employee,
    CostCenter
}
```

Labels are usually defined using an enumeration, but Neo4j just requires those labels that implement the `Label` interface.

> Labels are a very useful feature introduced in Neo4j 2.0 that allow us to label a node and make it easier to find them later. A node can have one or more labels, so you can express complex domain concepts. Labels can be indexed to improve the performance of a search as well.

We have three types of relationships:

- Employees that belong to cost centers
- Employees that report to other employees
- Employees that can be managers of a cost center

So, we have to define the relationships. This is usually done using the `enum` function, as shown in the following code snippet:

```
public enum EmployeeRelationship implements RelationshipType {
    REPORTS_TO,
    BELONGS_TO,
```

```
    MANAGER_OF;
    public static final String FROM = "from";
}
```

The FROM constant represents the name of a property. We will use it to store the start date of the validity of the relationship. Clearly, a real-world HR application would have a lot of relationships and properties; here we have just a subset.

# Creating nodes and relationships using the Java API

The next step is to fill in the database. First of all, to work with Neo4j using the Java API, we always need a transaction created from the GraphDatabaseService class. While building with Java 7, you can use the following syntax:

```
import org.neo4j.graphdb.Transaction;
import org.neo4j.graphdb.GraphDatabaseService;

// ...
try (Transaction tx = graphDb.beginTx()) {

    // work with the graph...
    tx.success();
}
```

The first line in the preceding code creates a transaction named tx. The call to success marks the transaction successful; every change will be committed once the transaction is closed. If an exception is thrown from inside the try statement, the transaction automatically ends with a rollback. When you use Java 6, the code is a little longer because you have to close the transaction explicitly within a finally clause, as shown in the following code:

```
Transaction tx = graphDb.beginTx();
try {
    // work with the graph...
    tx.success();
} finally {
    tx.close();
}
```

Now, in our application, cost centers are identified only by their code, while employees can have the following properties:

- Name
- Surname
- Middle name

Our relationships (REPORTS_TO, BELONGS_TO, and MANAGER_OF) can have a property (From) that specifies the dates of validity. The following code creates some examples of nodes and the relationships between them, and then sets the property values of nodes and some relationships:

```java
import java.util.GregorianCalendar;
import org.neo4j.graphdb.GraphDatabaseService;
import org.neo4j.graphdb.Node;
import org.neo4j.graphdb.Transaction;
import org.neo4j.graphdb.factory.GraphDatabaseFactory;

public class DatabaseSetup {

/**
* Properties of a cost center
*/
public static class CostCenter {
    public static final String CODE = "code";
}

/**
* Properties of an employee
*/
public static class Employee {
    public static final String NAME = "name";
    public static final String MIDDLE_NAME = "middleName";
    public static final String SURNAME = "surname";
}

Public static void setup(GraphDatabaseService graphDb) {

        try (Transaction tx = graphDb.beginTx()) {
            // set up of center costs
            Node cc1 = graphDb.createNode(HrLabels.CostCenter);
            cc1.setProperty(CostCenter.CODE, "CC1");

            Node cc2 = graphDb.createNode(HrLabels.CostCenter);
            cc2.setProperty(CostCenter. CODE, "CC2");

            Node davies = graphDb.createNode(HrLabels.Employee);
            davies.setProperty(Employee.NAME, "Nathan");
            davies.setProperty(Employee.SURNAME, "Davies");

            Node taylor = graphDb.createNode(HrLabels.Employee);
            taylor.setProperty(Employee.NAME, "Rose");
            taylor.setProperty(Employee.SURNAME, "Taylor");
```

```
Node underwood = graphDb.createNode(HrLabels.Employee);
underwood.setProperty(Employee.NAME, "Heather");
underwood.setProperty(Employee.MIDDLE_NAME, "Mary");
underwood.setProperty(Employee.SURNAME, "Underwood");

Node smith = graphDb.createNode(HrLabels.Employee);
smith.setProperty(Employee.NAME, "John");
smith.setProperty(Employee.SURNAME, "Smith");

// There is a vacant post in the company
Node vacantPost = graphDb.createNode();

// davies belongs to CC1
davies.createRelationshipTo(cc1, EmployeeRelationship.
BELONGS_TO)
            .setProperty(EmployeeRelationship.FROM,
                    new GregorianCalendar(2011, 1, 10).
getTimeInMillis());

// .. and reports to Taylor
davies.createRelationshipTo(taylor, EmployeeRelationship.
REPORTS_TO);

// Taylor is the manager of CC1
taylor.createRelationshipTo(cc1, EmployeeRelationship.
MANAGER_OF)
            .setProperty(EmployeeRelationship.FROM,
                    new GregorianCalendar(2010, 2,
8).getTimeInMillis());

// Smith belongs to CC2 from 2008
smith.createRelationshipTo(cc2, EmployeeRelationship.
BELONGS_TO)
            .setProperty(EmployeeRelationship.FROM,
                    new GregorianCalendar(2008, 9, 20).
getTimeInMillis());

// Smith reports to underwood
smith.createRelationshipTo(underwood,
EmployeeRelationship.REPORTS_TO);

// Underwood belongs to CC2
underwood.createRelationshipTo(cc2, EmployeeRelationship.
BELONGS_TO);

// Underwood will report to an employee not yet hired
underwood.createRelationshipTo(vacantPost,
EmployeeRelationship.REPORTS_TO);
```

```
            // But the vacant post will belong to CC2
            vacantPost.createRelationshipTo(cc2, EmployeeRelationship.
    BELONGS_TO);

            tx.success();
        }
    }
}
```

In the preceding code, we used the following functions of the `GraphDatabaseService` class:

- `createNode`: This creates a node and then returns it as result. The node will be created with a long, unique ID.

 Unlike relational databases, node IDs in Neo4j are not guaranteed to remain fixed forever. In fact, IDs are recomputed upon node deletion, so don't trust IDs, especially for long operations.

- `createRelationshipTo`: This creates a relationship between two nodes and returns that relationship in a relationship instance. This one too will have a long, unique ID.
- `setProperty`: This sets the value of a property of a node or a relationship.

We put the time in milliseconds in the property because Neo4j supports only the following types or an array of one of the following types:

- `boolean`
- `byte`
- `short`
- `int`
- `long`
- `float`
- `double`
- `String`

To store complex types of arrays, we can code them using the primitive types, as seen in the preceding list, but more often than not, the best approach is to create nodes. For example, if we have to store a property such as the entire address of a person, we can convert the address in JSON and store it as a string.

This way of storing data in a JSON format is common in document-oriented DBs, such as MongoDB, but since Neo4j isn't a document database, it won't build indexes on the properties of the document. So, for example, it would be difficult or very slow to query people by filtering on any field of the address, such as the ZIP code or the country. In other words, you should use this approach only for raw data that won't be filtered or processed with Cypher; in other cases, creating nodes is a better approach.

# A querying database

A typical report of our application is a list of all the employees. In our database, an employee is a node labeled `Employee`, so we have to find all nodes that match with the label `Employee` pattern. In Cypher, this can be expressed with the following query:

```
MATCH (e:Employee)
RETURN e
```

The `MATCH` clause introduces the pattern we are looking for. The `e:Employee` expression matches all `e` nodes that have the label `Employee`; this expression is within round brackets because `e` is a node. So, we have the first rule of matching expressions—node expressions must be within round brackets.

With the `RETURN` clause, we can specify what we want; for example, we can write a query to return the whole node with all its properties. In this clause, we can use any variable used in the `MATCH` clause. In the preceding query, we have specified that we want the whole node (with all its properties). If we are interested only in the name and the surname of the employees, we can make changes only in the `RETURN` clause:

```
MATCH (e:Employee)
RETURN e.name,e.surname
```

If any node does not have either of the properties, a `null` value is returned. This is a general rule for properties from version 2 of Cypher; missing properties are evaluated as `null` values.

The next question is how to invoke Cypher from Java.

# Invoking Cypher from Java

To execute Cypher queries on a Neo4j database, you need an instance of `ExecutionEngine`; this class is responsible for parsing and running Cypher queries, returning results in a `ExecutionResult` instance:

```
import org.neo4j.cypher.javacompat.ExecutionEngine;
import org.neo4j.cypher.javacompat.ExecutionResult;
```

```
// ...
ExecutionEngine engine =
  new ExecutionEngine(graphDb);
ExecutionResult result =
  engine.execute("MATCH (e:Employee) RETURN e");
```

Note that we use the `org.neo4j.cypher.javacompat` package and not the `org.neo4j.cypher` package even though they are almost the same. The reason is that Cypher is written in Scala, and Cypher authors provide us with the former package for better Java compatibility.

Now with the results, we can do one of the following options:

- Dumping to a string value
- Converting to a single column iterator
- Iterating over the full row

Dumping to a string is useful for testing purposes:

```
String dumped = result.dumpToString();
```

If we print the dumped string to the standard output stream, we will get the following result:

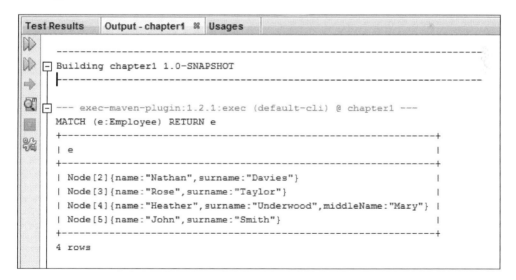

Here, we have a single column (**e**) that contains the nodes. Each node is dumped with all its properties. The numbers between the square brackets are the node IDs, which are the long and unique values assigned by Neo4j on the creation of the node.

When the result is a single column, or we need only one column of our result, we can get an iterator over one column with the following code:

```
import org.neo4j.graphdb.ResourceIterator;
// ...
ResourceIterator<Node> nodes = result.columnAs("e");
```

Then, we can iterate that column in the usual way, as shown in the following code:

```
while(nodes.hasNext()) {
    Node node = nodes.next();
    // do something with node
}
```

However, Neo4j provides a syntax-sugar utility to shorten the code that is to be iterated:

```
import org.neo4j.helpers.collection.IteratorUtil;
// ...
for (Node node : IteratorUtil.asIterable(nodes)) {
    // do something with node
}
```

If we need to iterate over a multiple-column result, we will write this code in the following way:

```
ResourceIterator<Map<String, Object>> rows = result.iterator();
for(Map<String,Object> row : IteratorUtil.asIterable(rows)) {
    Node n = (Node) row.get("e");
    try(Transaction t = n.getGraphDatabase().beginTx()) {
        // do something with node
    }
}
```

The `iterator` function returns an iterator of maps, where keys are the names of the columns. Note that when we have to work with nodes, even if they are returned by a Cypher query, we have to work in transaction. In fact, Neo4j requires that every time we work with the database, either reading or writing to the database, we must be in a transaction. The only exception is when we launch a Cypher query. If we launch the query within an existing transaction, Cypher will work as any other operation. No change will be persisted on the database until we commit the transaction, but if we run the query outside any transaction, Cypher will open a transaction for us and will commit changes at the end of the query.

# Finding nodes by relationships

If you have ever used the Neo4j Java API, you might wonder why we should write the following code:

```
ExecutionEngine engine =
   new ExecutionEngine(graphDb, StringLogger.SYSTEM);
ExecutionResult result =
   engine.execute("MATCH (e:Employee) RETURN e");
ResourceIterator<Node> nodes = result.columnAs("e");
```

You can get the same result with the Java API with a single line of code:

```
import org.neo4j.tooling.GlobalGraphOperations;
// ...
ResourceIterable<Node> empl = GlobalGraphOperations.at(graphDb)
                     .getAllNodesWithLabel(HrLabels.Employee);
```

However, pattern matching is much more powerful. By making slight changes to the query, we can get very important and different results; for example, we can find nodes that have relationships with other nodes. The query is as follows:

```
MATCH (n:Employee) --> (cc:CostCenter)
RETURN cc,n
```

The preceding query returns all employees that have a relation with any cost center:

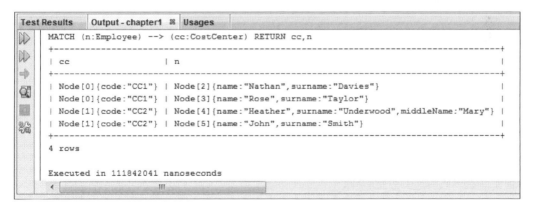

Again, as you can see, both n and cc are within round brackets. Here, the RETURN clause specifies both n and cc, which are the two columns returned. The result would be the same if we specified an asterisk instead of n and cc in the RETURN clause:

```
MATCH (n:Employee) --> (cc:CostCenter)
RETURN *
```

In fact, similar to SQL, the asterisk implies all the variables referenced in the patterns, but unlike SQL, not all properties of the entities are involved, just those of the referenced ones. In the previous query, relationships were not returned because we didn't put a variable in square brackets.

# Filtering properties

By making another slight change to the query, we can get all the employees that have a relation with a specific cost center, for example CC1. We have to filter the code property as shown in the following code:

```
MATCH (n:Employee) --> (:CostCenter { code: 'CC1' })
RETURN n
```

If we compare this query with the previous one, we can note three differences, which are listed as follows:

- The query returns only the employee node n because we don't care about the center cost here.
- Here, we omitted the cc variable. This is possible because we don't need to give a name to the cost center that matches the expression.
- In the second query, we added curly brackets in the cost center node to specify the property we are looking for. So, this is another rule of pattern-matching expressions: properties are expressed within curly brackets.

The --> symbol specifies the direction of the relation; in this case, outgoing from n. In the case of MATCH expressions, we can also use the <-- symbol for inverse direction. The following expression is exactly equivalent to the previous expression:

```
MATCH (:CostCenter { code: 'CC1' } ) <-- (n:Employee)
RETURN n
```

The preceding expression will give the same result:

```
+----------------------------------------+
| n                                      |
+----------------------------------------+
| Node[2]{name:"Nathan",surname:"Davies"} |
| Node[3]{name:"Rose",surname:"Taylor"}   |
+----------------------------------------+
```

If we don't have a preferred direction, we will use the -- symbol:

```
MATCH (n:Employee) -- (:CostCenter { code: 'CC1' } )
RETURN n
```

In our example, the latter query will return the same result as the previous one because in our model, relationships go from employees to cost centers.

# Filtering relationships

If we wish to know the existing relationships between the employees and cost centers, we will have to introduce another variable:

```
MATCH (n:Employee) -[r]- (:CostCenter { code: 'CC1' })
RETURN n.surname,n.name,r
```

The variable r matches any relationship that exists between the employees and cost center CC1 and is returned in a new column:

```
+-----------------------------------------------------------+
| n.surname | n.name  | r                                   |
+-----------------------------------------------------------+
| "Davies"  | "Nathan" | :BELONGS_TO[0]{from:1297292400000} |
| "Taylor"  | "Rose"   | :MANAGER_OF[2]{from:1268002800000} |
+-----------------------------------------------------------+
```

So, here we have the last rule: relationship expressions must be specified in square brackets.

To filter the employees who belong to a specific cost centre, we have to specify the relationship type:

```
MATCH (n) -[:BELONGS_TO]-> (:CostCenter { code: 'CC1' } )
RETURN n
```

This query matches any node n, which has a relation of the BELONGS_TO type with any node cc that has the value CC1 as a property code:

```
+---------------------------------------+
| n                                     |
+---------------------------------------+
| Node[2]{name:"Nathan",surname:"Davies"} |
+---------------------------------------+
```

We can specify multiple relationships using the | operator. The following query will search for all employees who belong to or are managers of the cost center CC1:

```
MATCH (n) -[r:BELONGS_TO|MANAGER_OF]-> (:CostCenter{code: 'CC1'})
RETURN n.name,n.surname,r
```

This time we returned only the name and surname, while the relationship is returned in the second column:

```
+-----------------------------------------------------------+
| n.name    | n.surname | r                                 |
+-----------------------------------------------------------+
|  "Nathan" |  "Davies" | :BELONGS_TO[0]{from:1297292400000} |
|  "Rose"   |  "Taylor" | :MANAGER_OF[2]{from:1268002800000} |
+-----------------------------------------------------------+
```

By making a slight change to the query in the preceding code, we can return the manager as well as the employees of the cost center as the result. This can be implemented as shown in the following query:

```
MATCH (n) -[:BELONGS_TO]-> (cc:CostCenter) <-[:MANAGER_OF]- (m)
RETURN n.surname,m.surname,cc.code
```

In this query, we can see the expressivity of Cypher—a very intuitive syntax to translate the "node n belonging to the cost center having a manager m" pattern. The result is the following code:

```
+--------------------------------+
| n.surname | m.surname | cc.code |
+--------------------------------+
| "Davies"  | "Taylor"  | "CC1"   |
+--------------------------------+
```

Of course, we can chain an increasing number of relationship expressions to describe very complex patterns:

```
MATCH (n) -[:BELONGS_TO]->
       (cc:CostCenter) <-[:MANAGER_OF]- (m) <-[:REPORTS_TO]- (k)
RETURN n.surname,m.surname,cc.code, k.surname
```

Another query that is very useful in real-world applications is finding nodes reachable from one node with a certain number of steps and a certain depth. The ability to execute this kind of query, and search the neighborhood, is one of the strong points of graph databases:

```
MATCH (:Employee {surname: 'Smith'}) -[*2]- (neighborhood)
RETURN neighborhood
```

This query returns the nodes that you can reach, starting from the `Davies` node, by visiting exactly two relationships of the graph. The result contains duplicated nodes because we have several paths to reach each of them:

```
+--------------------------------------------------------------------+
| neighborhood                                                       |
+--------------------------------------------------------------------+
| Node[4]{name:"Heather",surname:"Underwood",middleName:"Mary"}      |
| Node[6]{}                                                          |
| Node[1]{code:"CC2"}                                               |
| Node[6]{}                                                          |
+--------------------------------------------------------------------+
4 rows
```

> To get different values, we can use the `DISTINCT` keyword:
>
> ```
> MATCH (:Employee {surname: 'Smith'}) -[ *2]-
> (neighborhood)
> RETURN DISTINCT neighborhood
> ```

This time, we haven't specified any relationship type in the square brackets, so it matches any type. The expression `*2` means exactly two steps. With a little change, we can also ask for the relationships we visited:

```
MATCH (:Employee {surname: 'Davies'}) -[r*2]- (neighborhood)
RETURN neighborhood, r
```

Of course, by changing the number in the expression, we can get the query to navigate any number of relationships. However, we could also want all the nodes that are reachable from a number of relationships in a range of step numbers, for example, from two to three:

```
MATCH (:Employee {surname: 'Smith'}) -[r*2..3]- (neighborhood)
RETURN neighborhood,r
```

This is very useful in real-world applications such as social networks because it can be used to build lists, for example, a list of people you may know.

If we also want the starting node in the result, we can modify the range to start from `0`:

```
MATCH (:Employee{surname: 'Smith'}) -[r*0..2]- (neighborhood)
RETURN neighborhood,r
```

# Dealing with missing parts

In our applications, we often need to get some information related to something that could be missing. For example, if we want to get a list of all employees who have a specific number of employees reporting to them, then we must deal with those employees too who have no employees reporting to them. In fact, we can write:

```
MATCH (e:Employee) <-[:REPORTS_TO]- (m:Employee)
RETURN e.surname,m.surname
```

From this, the following result is obtained:

```
+-----------------------+
| e.surname  | m.surname |
+-----------------------+
| "Taylor"    | "Davies"  |
| "Underwood" | "Smith"   |
+-----------------------+
```

However, this is not what we are looking for. In fact, we want all the employees, with all the employees that report to them as an option. This type of relation is similar to the OUTER JOIN clause of SQL and can be done in Cypher using OPTIONAL MATCH. This keyword allows us to use any pattern expression that can be used in the MATCH clause, but it describes only a pattern that could match. If the pattern does not match, the OPTIONAL MATCH clause sets any variable to null variable:

```
MATCH (e:Employee)
OPTIONAL MATCH (e) <-[:REPORTS_TO]- (m:Employee)
RETURN e.surname,m.surname, c.code
```

In this query, we slightly changed the previous one; we just inserted OPTIONAL MATCH (e). The effect is that the first part (e:Employee) must match, but the pattern following OPTIONAL MATCH may or may not match. So, this query returns any employee e, and if e has a relationship of the REPORTS_TO type with any other employee, this query is returned in m; otherwise, m will be a null value. The result is as follows:

```
+--------------------------+
| e.surname   | m.surname  |
+--------------------------+
| "Davies"    | <null>     |
| "Taylor"    | "Davies"   |
| "Underwood" | "Smith"    |
| "Smith"     | <null>     |
+--------------------------+
```

Unlike object-oriented languages where referencing any property of a null object will result in a null-reference exception, in Cypher referencing, which is a property of the null node, we get a `null` value again.

Now, let's say that we also want to know whether the employee is the manager of any center cost, and if so, which one. Also, we want to know the cost center of any employee. For this, we can write the following code:

```
MATCH (e:Employee)
OPTIONAL MATCH (c:CostCenter) <-[:MANAGER_OF]- (e) <-[:REPORTS_TO]-
(m:Employee)
RETURN e.surname,m.surname
```

The preceding code returns the following result:

```
+-----------------------------------+
| e.surname   | m.surname | c.code  |
+-----------------------------------+
| "Davies"    | <null>    | <null>  |
| "Taylor"    | "Davies"  | "CC1"   |
| "Underwood" | <null>    | <null>  |
| "Smith"     | <null>    | <null>  |
+-----------------------------------+
```

What happened? Does it look like `Smith` does not report to `Underwood` anymore? This weird result is due to the fact that the whole pattern in `OPTIONAL MATCH` must match. We can't have partially matched patterns. Since we can add as many `OPTIONAL MATCH` expressions as we want to, we have to write the following code to get the result we are looking for:

```
MATCH (e:Employee)
OPTIONAL MATCH (e) <-[:REPORTS_TO]- (m:Employee)
OPTIONAL MATCH (e) -[:MANAGER_OF]-> (c:CostCenter)
RETURN e.surname, m.surname, c.code
```

In fact, the result is the following code:

```
+-----------------------------------+
| e.surname   | m.surname | c.code  |
+-----------------------------------+
| "Davies"    | <null>    | <null>  |
| "Taylor"    | "Davies"  | "CC1"   |
| "Underwood" | "Smith"   | <null>  |
| "Smith"     | <null>    | <null>  |
+-----------------------------------+
```

This query works because we have two OPTIONAL MATCH clauses that can independently generate a successful match.

# Working with paths

As we have seen earlier, graph databases are useful to find paths between two nodes:

```
MATCH path = (a{surname:'Davies'}) -[*]- (b{surname:'Taylor'})
RETURN path
```

This query uses a construct which we have not used so far—the path assignment, path =. The assignment of variables can be done only with paths. Note that the query in the preceding code returns all the possible paths from two nodes. Here, the result is two paths in our database:

```
[Node[2]{name:"Nathan",surname:"Davies"},:BELONGS_TO[0]
{from:1297292400000},Node[0]{code:"CC1"},:MANAGER_OF[2]
{from:1268002800000},Node[3]{name:"Rose",surname:"Taylor"}] |
  [Node[2]{name:"Nathan",surname:"Davies"},:REPORTS_TO[1]{},Node[3]
{name:"Rose",surname:"Taylor"}]
```

However, what if we need the shortest path between them? The shortest path is the path with the least number of nodes visited. Clearly, we could iterate over all the paths and take the shortest, but Cypher provides a function that does the work for us:

```
MATCH (a{surname:'Davies'}), (b{surname:'Taylor'})
RETURN allShortestPaths((a)-[*]-(b)) as path
```

Let's see what is new in this query:

- MATCH: In this clause, we have two node expressions (in round brackets) separated by a comma. These expressions, a and b, match any node independently, just like a Cartesian product.

- RETURN: In this clause, we have to call the allShortestPath function that takes an expression as a parameter. The expression is a variable length relation (this is the asterisk between the square brackets). Here, we don't care about relationship types and the direction, but we can filter properties, relation types involved, and so on, if necessary.

- RETURN: In this clause, we have an alias. An alias must be defined using the keyword AS. It just specifies the name of the column returned.

## Node IDs as starting points

When we execute a query like the previous code, Cypher must find the nodes and relationships that match the pattern. However, to do so, it must start to search from a set of nodes or relationships. We can let Cypher find the starting points of a query on its own, but we can also specify them because we want to search a pattern that starts from a specific node, or a specific relation resulting in an important improvement in the performances of the query.

We can assign starting points to variables in the query using the START keyword. The previous query, for example, could be rewritten in the following way:

```
START a=node(2), b=node(3)
RETURN allShortestPaths((a)-[*]-(b)) AS path
```

If we execute this query, and compare the time elapsed in executing this query and the previous one, we can easily prove that the latter is dramatically faster. The drawback is that we need to know the ID of the node.

# Query parameters

In real-world applications, you often need to execute a query multiple times, changing a value in the query every time. For example, you need to find an employee by the surname, but the surname is typed by the application user from the keyboard. Cypher allows us to use parameters, just like in SQL. The names of the parameters must be between curly brackets:

```
MATCH (n:Employee {surname: {inputSurname} })
RETURN n
```

In this query, we have a parameter (inputSurname), whose value must be provided while executing the query.

## Passing parameters with Java

The Cypher Java API wants us to pass all the parameters in the map. The following code is a class example that has a public method to find all employees by their surname:

```
import java.util.Map;
import java.util.HashMap;
import org.neo4j.cypher.javacompat.ExecutionEngine;
import org.neo4j.cypher.javacompat.ExecutionResult;
import org.neo4j.graphdb.Node;
import org.neo4j.helpers.collection.IteratorUtil;
```

```
public class EmployeeRepository {

    public Iterator<Node> bySurname(String surname) {
        Map<String, Object> params = new HashMap<>();
        params.put("inputSurname", surname);
        ExecutionResult result = engine
            .execute("MATCH (n:Employee {surname: {inputSurname}})" +
                    "RETURN n",
                    params);
        Iterator<Node> nodes = result.columnAs("n");
        return nodes;
    }
}
```

The bySurname method takes the surname of the employees as a parameter to search, and it creates a new HashMap and puts the parameter in the map. Finally, the map is passed to the execute method of ExecutionEngine, and the result is treated in the usual way.

 Since parameters are referenced by name, you can reference the same variable several times in the query.

# Summary

In this chapter, you first created a Neo4j database using the Java API. It details how Neo4j works with nodes and relationships.

Then, you queried that database to learn Cypher pattern matching. You learned about the MATCH keyword. You also learned that node expressions must go between round brackets, while relationships must be expressed in square brackets, and property expressions must be written between curly brackets.

You also learned how to use the RETURN clause to select which matched values we want the query to return. We wrote the Java code needed to use the result, even using query parameters. The OPTIONAL MATCH keyword allows us to match parts of the graph that could be missing. You also learned how to find paths from one node to another, and the shortest path between them, using the allShortestPaths function.

In the next chapter, you will learn how to filter and aggregate data and how to page through a query result.

# 2
# Filter, Aggregate, and Combine Results

In the previous chapter, we learned the basics of Cypher querying, including pattern matching. To use Cypher in real-world applications, you'll need a set of features, which we are going to cover in this chapter. These features include searching by text in the database, data aggregation for statistical analysis, pagination for performance improvements, or even simple filtering on an array of properties.

## Filtering

Pattern matching is useful to describe the data we are looking for and how nodes and relations are organized in the graph database. However, we often need to filter data in more detail.

## The book store – an example

In this chapter, we'll learn how to filter results using a real-world example: the book store. Just as we saw in the previous chapter, we have to define labels and relationships. A minimal set of labels are as follows:

- **Book**: This label includes all the books
- **Person**: This label includes authors, translators, reviewers, and so on
- **Publisher**: This label includes the publishers of books in the database
- **User**: This label includes the users of the website

A set of basic relationships are as follows:

- **PublishedBy**: This relationship is used to specify that a book was published by a publisher
- **Votes**: This relationship describes the relation between a user and a book, for example, how a book was rated by a user

Every book has the following properties:

- **Title**: This is the title of the book in string format
- **Tags**: This is an array of string tags useful for searching through the database based on topic, arguments, geographic regions, languages, and so on

Now, suppose we have already filled the database with a lot of books, and we are developing the website of the book store. In such applications, providing an effective search is very important because we can't make the user scroll through all the results on their own.

In the example code files that you can download from the Packt Publishing website at `http://www.packtpub.com/support`, you'll find an example database that contains 150 books. I used this database to perform the queries in this chapter. The graph of this example database can be seen in the following screenshot:

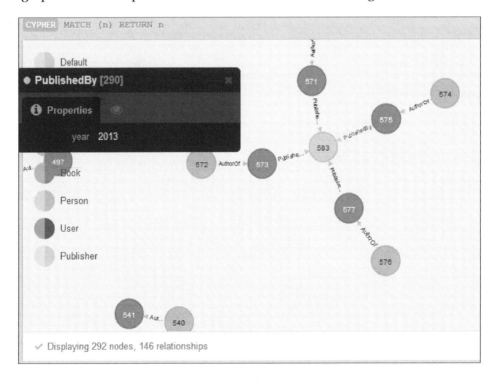

# Text search

In the previous chapter, we saw that we can search a node or a relationship with a given value of a property. Of course, this is very useful when you know that a certain node with a given value of a property exists; this is the case when a user is looking for a book and knows its title exactly. Consider the following query:

```
MATCH (b:Book { title: 'In Search of Lost Time' })
RETURN b
```

The same query can be written using the WHERE keyword, as shown in the following query:

```
MATCH (b:Book)
WHERE b.title = 'In Search of Lost Time'
RETURN b
```

In fact, for both queries, the result is as follows:

```
+-----------------------------------------------------------+
| b                                                         |
+-----------------------------------------------------------+
| Node[143]{title:"In Search of Lost Time",tags:["novel"]} |
+-----------------------------------------------------------+
```

WHERE is the keyword that introduces a filter predicate; in this case, a filter based on the equality comparison of a property (Book.title) and a value (the text to search).

Note that the preceding two queries, although being quite different, have exactly the same effect and the same performance results because they are interpreted in the same way by the engine. This means that choosing either syntax is just a matter of taste. The latter is more similar to SQL. In fact, the creators of Cypher were inspired by SQL when they introduced the WHERE clause.

# Working with regular expressions

Maybe in a real-world application, this kind of search would be performed in an advanced search section of a website. In fact, the common search by title function would look for titles that contain the text typed by the user. With Cypher, this can be done with regular expressions.

Regular expressions are widely used patterns that match expressions for strings. The following query will match all titles that contain the word Lost:

```
MATCH (b:Book)
WHERE b.title =~ '.*Lost.*'
RETURN b
```

Here, the special character . matches any character, while * matches any occurrence of the previous pattern, and once combined, .* matches any occurrence of any character. So, the regular expression .*Lost.* matches all strings that contain any character at the beginning (.*), then the word Lost and finally, any other character (.*). The result of this query is as follows:

```
+-------------------------------------------------------------------+
| b                                                                 |
+-------------------------------------------------------------------+
| Node[143]{title:"In Search of Lost Time",tags:["novel"]}          |
| Node[221]{title:"Love's Labour's Lost",tags:["comedy","drama"]}|
+-------------------------------------------------------------------+
```

With regular expressions, of course, we can do much more. Just to remind us how regular expressions work, the following is a table of the most widely used patterns:

| Pattern | Meaning | Example | Matched Strings |
|---|---|---|---|
| [] | This stands for any character included in the bracket or in the range specified | Te[sx]t<br><br>[A-C]lt | Text Test<br><br>Alt Blt Clt |
| * | This implies any occurrence of the preceding pattern, including no occurrence | Te[xs]*t | Text Test Texxt Tet |
| . | This implies any character, including none | Te.t | Text Test |
| ? | This implies one or no occurrence of the preceding pattern | Te[xs]?t | Text Test Tet |
| \| | This stands for alternative matching | Te(xt\|ll) | Text Tell |
| \ | This pattern escapes the following reserved character | Te\.t | Te.t |

The regular expression standard used here is identical to the one used by Java in the official Java documentation at http://docs.oracle.com/javase/6/docs/api/java/util/regex/Pattern.html. There, you can find the full summary of the constructs supported.

The following is a list of some of the most widely used regular expression patterns:

| Regular expression | Matches |
|---|---|
| `([a-z0-9_\.-]+)@([\da-z\.-]+)\.([a-z\.]{2,6})` | E-mail |
| `(https?:\/\/)?([\da-z\.-]+)\.([a-z\.]{2,6})([\/\w \.-]*)*\/?` | An HTTP URL without a query string |
| `<([a-z]+)([^<]+)*(?:>(.*)<\/\1>|\s+\/>)` | HTML tags |
| `\d{5}` | A ZIP code |
| `\+?[\d\s]{3,}` | A phone number |

So, if we are looking for all titles that start with a given text (for example, Henry), we can write the following query:

```
MATCH (b:Book)
WHERE b.title =~ 'Henry.*'
RETURN b
```

The following query returns all the books that have *tale*, *tales*, or their respective title cases:

```
MATCH (b:Book)
WHERE b.title =~ '.*[Tt]ale(s)?.*'
RETURN b
```

The result is shown in the following output code:

```
+-----------------------------------------------------------------+
| b                                                               |
+-----------------------------------------------------------------+
| Node[3]{title:"Fairy tales"}                                    |
| Node[31]{title:"The Canterbury Tales"}                          |
| Node[129]{title:"The Tale of Genji"}                            |
| Node[141]{title:"Tales"}                                        |
| Node[245]{title:"The Winter's Tale",tags:["comedy","drama"]}    |
+-----------------------------------------------------------------+
```

By design, regular expressions are case sensitive. If you want to match a string independently by a letter's case, you can use the `(?i)` specifier. Place it at the beginning of the string to perform case-insensitive matching. The following query gives the same result as the previous one with respect to our database:

```
MATCH (b:Book)
WHERE b.title =~ '(?i).*tale(s)?.*'
RETURN b
```

You can find a lot of free resources online on regular expressions. Apart from the official Oracle documentation, you can find a lot of reading material on the following websites:

- `http://www.rexegg.com/`: This is a tutorial with links and examples
- `http://www.regexplanet.com/advanced/java/index.html`: This is a tester that uses the `java.util.regex.Pattern` implementation
- `https://www.addedbytes.com/cheat-sheets/regular-expressions-cheat-sheet/`: This is a comprehensive cheat sheet

# Escaping the text

In real-world applications, sometimes we have to use regular expression patterns dynamically; for example, we will use the following code snippet while working in Java:

```
String query = "(?i).*" + textToFind;
Map<String, Object> params = new HashMap<>();
params.put("query", query);
ExecutionResult result = engine
    .execute("MATCH (b:Book) WHERE b.title =~ {query} RETURN b",
        params);
```

This code puts the `textToFind` string in a regular expression pattern, which is then passed to the query as a parameter.

The problem with this code is that if `textToFind` comes from the user input (as it's quite likely), a user could type in a valid regular expression pattern and still get an unexpected result. For example, the word *10$* would match only the titles that end with *10* and not all the titles that contain the word *10$*.

In Java, escaping the text is easy, as shown in the following code snippet:

```
import java.util.regex.Pattern;
String query = "(?i).*" + Pattern.quote(textToFind);
```

Of course, every programming language or environment has its own functions to escape regular expressions. You should refer to their respective documentation.

# Value comparisons

We often need to search items by comparing their values. For example, if we want all books published in 2012 and later, this can be done as follows:

```
MATCH (b:Book) -[r:PublishedBy]-> (:Publisher)
WHERE r.year >= 2012
RETURN b.title, r.year
```

This query matches all book nodes that have a relation with a publisher, filtering the books by comparing their year of publication, which must be greater than or equal to 2012. The result is shown in the following output code:

```
+------------------------------------------+
| book.title                   | r.year |
+------------------------------------------+
| "Akka Essentials"             | 2012   |
| "Getting Started with Memcached" | 2013   |
| "Java EE 7 Developer Handbook"   | 2013   |
+------------------------------------------+
```

The >= is a comparison operator. The other comparison operators are as follows:

- <>: This is the different than operator
- <: This is the lesser than operator
- <=: This is the lesser than or equal to operator
- >: This is the greater than operator

 You can find the complete list of supported operators and functions, each explained with an example, in the *Appendix*.

# The IN predicate

The IN predicate allows us to specify more values for an expression. For example, consider the following query:

```
MATCH (b:Book) -[r:PublishedBy]-> (:Publisher)
WHERE r.year IN [2012, 2013]
RETURN b.title, r.year
```

This query matches all books published in 2012 or in 2013. It's a short alternative for the Boolean operator OR, which can be used as shown in the following query:

```
r.year = 2012 OR r.year = 2013
```

## Boolean operators

The WHERE clause supports four Boolean operators. They are as follows:

- OR: This is the logical inclusive disjunction operator.

- AND: This is the logical conjunction operator; it returns TRUE only if both predicates are TRUE.

- XOR: This is the logical exclusive disjunction operator; it returns TRUE if only one of the predicates is TRUE. Use this if you don't want the results to satisfy both the predicates.

- NOT: This operator returns TRUE only if the following predicate is FALSE.

# Working with collections

In *Chapter 1, Querying Neo4j Effectively with Pattern Matching*, we saw that Neo4j supports array parameters. So, how can we filter nodes and relationships by array values?

Collection predicates are functions with a predicate argument that return a Boolean value. Suppose you want to get all books that have a particular tag from a given dataset. With collection predicates, we can filter books based on collections.

For example, if we have tagged every book with an array of strings, the query will be as follows:

```
MATCH (b:Book)
WHERE ANY ( tag IN b.tags WHERE tag IN ['nosql','neo4j'] )
RETURN b.title,b.tags
```

The preceding query returns all books tagged with NoSQL, Neo4j, or both. The following result is obtained:

```
+-------------------------------------------------------------------+
| b.title                           | b.tags                        |
+-------------------------------------------------------------------+
| "Getting Started with NoSQL"      | ["nosql"]                     |
| "Learning Cypher"                 | ["nosql","neo4j"]             |
| "Instant MongoDB"                 | ["nosql","mongodb"]           |
| "Ruby and MongoDB Web Development" | ["nosql","mongodb","ruby"]|
+-------------------------------------------------------------------+
```

How does this query work? The keyword ANY, just as every predicate, introduces a rule with the following syntax:

```
item_identifier IN collection WHERE rule
```

In the case of ANY, at least one item in the collections must follow the rule. So, for every book, if there is any tag in the collection that satisfies the rule, it will be taken; otherwise, it will be discarded.

There are four collection predicates. They are as follows:

- ANY: This predicate returns TRUE if at least one item in the collection adheres to the expression
- ALL: This predicate returns TRUE if all items in the collection adhere to the rule
- NONE: This predicate returns TRUE if no item in the collection follows the rule
- SINGLE: This predicate returns TRUE if exactly one item follows the rule

For example, if we want books tagged only as Neo4j or NoSQL and nothing else, we have to change the previous query as follows:

```
MATCH (b:Book)
WHERE ALL( tag IN b.tags WHERE tag IN ['nosql','neo4j'] )
RETURN b.title, b.tags
```

Note that we have just replaced the ANY keyword with the ALL keyword, and we get the following result:

```
+--------------------------------------------------+
| b.title                    | b.tags              |
+--------------------------------------------------+
| "Getting Started with NoSQL" | ["nosql"]         |
| "Learning Cypher"          | ["nosql","neo4j"]   |
+--------------------------------------------------+
```

If we want all books tagged as NoSQL but not as Neo4j, we can use the NONE predicate as follows:

```
MATCH (b:Book)
WHERE ANY  ( tag IN b.tags WHERE tag = 'nosql' )
  AND NONE ( tag in b.tags WHERE tag = 'neo4j' )
RETURN b.title,b.tags
```

In fact, the result does not contain any book that is tagged `Neo4j`, as shown in the following output code:

```
+------------------------------------------------------------------+
| b.title                              | b.tags                    |
+------------------------------------------------------------------+
| "Getting Started with NoSQL"         | ["nosql"]                 |
| "Instant MongoDB"                    | ["nosql","mongodb"]       |
| "Ruby and MongoDB Web Development"   | ["nosql","mongodb","ruby"]|
+------------------------------------------------------------------+
```

The `SINGLE` predicate is useful for performing the exclusive-OR operation among collection values. For example, if we want all books tagged either `Ruby` or `MongoDB` (we don't want too specific books), we will use the following code:

```
MATCH (b:Book)
WHERE SINGLE (tag IN b.tags WHERE tag IN ('ruby', ' mongodb ')
   )
RETURN b
```

The preceding query works because if we have a book tagged both `Ruby` and `MongoDB`, the `SINGLE` statement won't match because the specified predicate will return two tags. The result is shown in the following output code:

```
+------------------------------------------+
| b.title            | b.tags              |
+------------------------------------------+
| "Instant MongoDB"  | ["nosql","mongodb"] |
+------------------------------------------+
```

# Paging results – LIMIT and SKIP

Even if you have never developed a web application, you would know why paging results is so important, for the following reasons:

- Loading a lot of data in a single HTTP request is very slow
- Showing a lot of data in a single page is very expensive in terms of bandwidth

Paging is necessary to avoid a lot of data from being loaded all together in a single query. For example, if the user searches for the string *drama* in the book database, the full result would likely be huge, that is, hundreds of books. Here, we can split the result in pages of twenty books; we can show twenty books in each page and have two buttons, next and previous, to switch the page forward or backward.

We get the first page with the following query:

```
MATCH (b:Book)
WHERE b.title =~ '(?i).*drama.*'
RETURN b
LIMIT 20
```

This will return the first twenty nodes with the `Book` label that have the title that matches the regular expression `(?i).*drama.*`. The `(?i)` part of the expression means that the regular expression is case insensitive, while the `.*` part of the expression matches any character type in the string. So, the regular expression matches every string that contains the word *drama*, independent of the character case.

Now, when the user clicks on the "next" button, we have to get the second chunk of data, skipping the first part. We must use the `SKIP` keyword as shown in the following query:

```
MATCH (b:Book)
WHERE b.title =~ '(?i).*drama.*'
RETURN b
SKIP 20
LIMIT 20
```

To get the third chunk of data, we have to skip past the first 40 items and so on for further pages; to show the page *i*, we must skip *20\*i* items. To avoid having to change the query every time, we can take advantage of the Cypher parameters, as shown in the following query:

```
MATCH (b:Book)
WHERE b.title =~ {query}
RETURN b
SKIP {skip}
LIMIT {limit}
```

The preceding query uses three parameters: `query`, `skip`, and `limit`. The first is the regular expression to find in the title, and the others are the number of items to skip and to return.

Using the REST API, a call using the paginated query will have the following payload:

```
{
  "query" : "MATCH (b:Book) WHERE b.title =~ {query} RETURN b SKIP
    {skip} LIMIT {limit}",
  "params" : {
    "query" : "(?i).*drama.*",
```

```
      "skip" : 20,
      "limit": 20
   }
}
```

Whereas in a Java-embedded database, the query can be used in a method as shown in the following code snippet:

```java
import java.util.*;
import java.util.regex.Pattern;
import org.neo4j.cypher.javacompat.*;
import org.neo4j.graphdb.Node;
import org.neo4j.helpers.collection.IteratorUtil;

// ... more code

public List<Node> find(String text, int limit, int skip) {
   final String query = "(?i).*" + Pattern.quote(text) + ".*";

   Map<String, Object> params = new HashMap<>();
   params.put("query", query);
   params.put("limit", limit);
   params.put("skip", skip);

   final ExecutionResult result = engine
      .execute("MATCH (b:Book) WHERE b.title =~ {query} RETURN b
        SKIP {skip} LIMIT {limit}", params);
   List<BNode> ret = new LinkedList<>();

   Iterator<Node> iterator = result.columnAs("b");
   for(Node b : IteratorUtil.asIterable(iterator)) {
      ret.add(b);
   }
   return ret;
}
```

This is the basic method to perform text searches in the database in order to show items in the graphical user interface. It takes three parameters: the text to find, the maximum number of items to return, and the number of items to skip. Then, it puts them in a map used as the parameter list in the following query:

```
MATCH (b:Book) WHERE b.title =~ {query} RETURN b SKIP {skip} LIMIT
{limit}
```

Finally, the result is put in a list and returned. Maybe you are wondering if you can sort the results before paging the data. This is possible and important because you can use this feature, for example, to return the top ten most-voted books. This is the topic of the next section.

# Sorting

If you have experience with SQL, then sorting with Cypher is exactly the same as sorting with SQL. We can use the ORDER BY clause to specify the columns to be used for sorting, as shown in the following query:

```
MATCH (b:Book)
WHERE ANY ( tag IN b.tags WHERE tag IN ['drama'] )
RETURN b.title
ORDER BY b.title
LIMIT 5
```

The preceding query looks for books tagged drama in the database, then sorts them by title, and returns the first five book entries found. We can note the following:

- The ORDER BY clause follows the RETURN clause
- This clause is above the LIMIT or SKIP clause so that we can sort the data before limiting our page

The result set is as follows:

```
+-----------------------------+
| b.title                     |
+-----------------------------+
| "A Lover's Complaint"       |
| "A Midsummer Night's Dream" |
| "All's Well That Ends Well" |
| "Anthony and Cleopatra"     |
| "As You Like It"            |
+-----------------------------+
```

# A descending sort

To sort inversely, just postpone the DESC clause to the ORDER BY clause, as shown as shown in the following query:

```
MATCH (b:Book)
WHERE ANY ( tag IN b.tags WHERE tag IN ['drama'] )
```

```
RETURN b.title
ORDER BY b.title DESC
LIMIT 5
```

It gives the following result:

```
+-----------------------+
| b.title               |
+-----------------------+
| "Venus and Adonis"    |
| "Twelfth Night"       |
| "Troilus and Cressida"|
| "Titus Andronicus"    |
| "Timon of Athens"     |
+-----------------------+
```

The result rows are different because the LIMIT clause is evaluated after the ORDER BY clause, so Cypher is limiting the result set to five items, which are already sorted. This is important in real-world applications because it allows us to both page data in a small result set and sort it however we want.

# Dealing with null values using the COALESCE function

How are null values evaluated by the ORDER BY clause? They are always considered the largest values; so, they are the last values in case of an ascending sort, while they are the first values in case of a descending sort. This is useful while we are looking for data that is sorted in an ascending manner, and indeed that's likely to be the most common situation. But with a descending sort, we can get unexpected results.

The following query returns books from our database, putting the most recently published books at the top:

```
MATCH (b:Book)
OPTIONAL MATCH (b) -[p:PublishedBy]-> (c)
RETURN b.title, p.year
ORDER BY p.year DESC
LIMIT 5
```

We are using an OPTIONAL MATCH clause because we want to get all the books in the database, but as the database does not contain the publication year for some books, we get them at the first position:

```
+-----------------------------+
| b.title            | p.year |
+-----------------------------+
| "Fairy tales"       | <null> |
| "The Divine Comedy" | <null> |
| "Epic of Gilgamesh" | <null> |
| "Book of Job"       | <null> |
| "The Art of Prolog" | <null> |
+-----------------------------+
```

So, how to get the null values to stay at the bottom of the list and the most recent book at the top?

For this, COALESCE is the function we need. It takes a variable number of arguments and returns the first non-null value. A null value is returned only if all arguments are null.

Using the COALESCE function, we can write the preceding query in the ORDER BY clause as follows:

```
MATCH (b:Book)
OPTIONAL MATCH (b) -[p:PublishedBy]-> (c)
RETURN b.title, p.year
ORDER BY COALESCE(p.year, -5000) DESC
LIMIT 5
```

Here, we have instructed Cypher to sort the dataset by a value, that is, the year of publication. If it is a null value, it is considered as -5000. Now, we have the result we were expecting, as shown in the following output code:

```
+-------------------------------------------+
| b.title                        | p.year  |
+-------------------------------------------+
| "Getting Started with Memcached" | 2013   |
| "Java EE 7 Developer Handbook"   | 2013   |
| "Akka Essentials"                | 2012   |
| "Learning Ext JS 3.2"            | 2010   |
| "The Art of Prolog"              | <null> |
+-------------------------------------------+
```

# Aggregating results

In our application, we have users who rate books with a score from one to five. Now, we are going to query the database to get some aggregated information about book scores.

## Counting matching rows or non-null values

Suppose that we want to know the number of users who have voted for a book. For this, we need to count the number of the vote relations between the users and that book, as shown in the following code snippet:

```
START b=node({id})
MATCH (b) <-[r:Vote]- (u:User)
RETURN COUNT(*) as votes
```

The only difference with the query patterns we already know is that here, we have used the COUNT function in the RETURN clause. With Cypher, the RETURN clause drives the aggregation of entities. In this case, as we have nothing else in the RETURN clause but the COUNT function, all the matching results are counted and the result is a single value. The result is as shown in the following output code:

```
+-------+
| votes |
+-------+
| 7     |
+-------+
1 row
```

The arguments inside the COUNT function can be the following:

- The * keyword is a placeholder that instructs the counter to count all matching rows
- A variable that makes the counter skip null values, missing properties, or missing matches

In the previous query, specifying the COUNT(r.score) score property will give the same result because in our database, we haven't got any null votes. However, we can have a book without any scores. Now, we are going to investigate two queries that differ only in the usage of the COUNT function. The first query is as follows:

```
MATCH (b:Book {title: "The Art of Prolog"})
OPTIONAL MATCH (b) <-[r:Votes]- (:User)
RETURN b, COUNT(r.score) as votes
```

The preceding query counts only the rows that have a non-null vote score. The following result is obtained:

```
+------------------------------------------------------------+
| b                                              | votes |
+------------------------------------------------------------+
| Node[1037]{title:"The Art of Prolog",tags:["prolog"]} | 0     |
+------------------------------------------------------------+
```

We have no votes here because no user has voted for this book. Now, look at the following query where I have changed COUNT(r.score) to COUNT(*):

```
MATCH (b:Book {title: "The Art of Prolog"})
OPTIONAL MATCH (b) <-[r:Votes]- (:User)
RETURN b, COUNT(*) as votes
```

This query gives one vote in the result, as shown in the following output code:

```
+------------------------------------------------------------+
| b                                              | votes |
+------------------------------------------------------------+
| Node[1037]{title:"The Art of Prolog",tags:["prolog"]} | 1     |
+------------------------------------------------------------+
```

In fact, we are using the COUNT(*) function to count all the rows that match the expression in the first row of the query. We have just one matching row because the presence of the votes relationship is optional. So, we have this matching row counted as one vote, which of course is wrong.

> Be careful while using the COUNT(*) function versus the COUNT(variable) function, in conjunction with the OPTIONAL MATCH clause; you could get unexpected results!

# Summation

If you are interested in the total score received by a book too, you can use the SUM function, as shown in the following query:

```
START b=node(5)
MATCH (b:Book) <-[r:Votes]- (:User)
RETURN COUNT(r.score) as votes, SUM(r.score) as total
```

The argument of the SUM function is the variable to summarize. The result of this query is as follows:

```
+---------------+
| votes | total |
+---------------+
| 5     | 14    |
+---------------+
```

Here, the null values will be ignored.

# Average

The average score is the sum of all the scores given by the users on a book divided by the sum of the number of votes. The AVG function computes this for us, as shown in the following query:

```
START b=node(5)
MATCH (b:Book) <-[r:Votes]- (:User)
RETURN AVG(r.score) as avgScore
```

The argument of this function is the variable whose average we want to compute. Here too, the null values will be ignored.

 The AVG function treats null values differently from zero. A zero is summed in the average and counted, while null values are just ignored. null values don't influence the average. For example, the average of 10 and a null value will be 10, while the average of 10 and 0 will be 5.

The result of the previous query is as follows:

```
+-----------+
| avgScore  |
+-----------+
| 3.8       |
+-----------+
```

Note that although our score data consisted of integer values, the AVG function returns a floating point value (double).

# Maximum and minimum

Cypher provides the functions MAX and MIN to compute the largest and the smallest value in the property specified as argument, respectively. Consider the following query:

```
START b=node(5)
MATCH (b:Book) <-[r:Votes]- (:User)
RETURN MAX(r.score), MIN(r.score)
```

This query returns the largest and the smallest score vote given to the book. The result is as shown in the following output code:

```
+----------------------------+
| MAX(r.score) | MIN(r.score) |
+----------------------------+
| 5            | 3            |
+----------------------------+
```

Again, null values are ignored.

# Standard deviation

The standard deviation measures the variation from average for a set of values. In our case, it will predict how many voters agree about the average score. Consider the following query:

```
START b=node(5)
MATCH (b:Book) <-[r:Votes]- (:User)
RETURN AVG(r.score) as avgScore, STDEV(r.score) as stdDevScore
```

The preceding query returns the standard deviation with the average. The result is as follows:

```
+----------------------------+
| avgScore | stdDevScore      |
+----------------------------+
| 3.8      | 0.8366600265340756 |
+----------------------------+
```

The result tells us that the average is 3.8 and that users agree with the votes.

Cypher also provides other statistical aggregation functions. You can find explanations on them in the *Appendix*.

# Collecting values in an array

If statistical functions provided by Cypher are not enough for your needs, you can collect all the values in an array so that you can easily process them with your preferred algorithm. For example, the following query returns all the score votes received for two books:

```
START b=node(5,6)
MATCH (b:Book) <-[r:Votes]- (:User)
RETURN b.title, COLLECT(r.score)
```

As you can see, we used the START keyword to instruct Cypher to start from two nodes, those with the ID 5 or ID 6, and for each of them, we got the collected values of scores. The result is shown in the following output code:

```
+--------------------------------------+
| b.title               | COLLECT(r.score) |
+--------------------------------------+
| "Epic of Gilgamesh"   | [5,4,3,4,1]      |
| "The Divine Comedy"   | [4,3,5,3,4]      |
+--------------------------------------+
```

# Grouping keys

To better explain how the RETURN function works with aggregation, let's try to remove the b.title column. The query would then be as follows:

```
START b=node(5,6)
MATCH (b:Book) <-[r:Votes]- (:User)
RETURN COLLECT(r.score)
```

The result is strongly different from the result of the preceding query, as shown in the following output code:

```
+----------------------+
| COLLECT(r.score)     |
+----------------------+
| [3,3,5,2,1,4,3,1,1,3] |
+----------------------+
```

In fact, the purpose of the b.title column in the previous query was to set a grouping key of the rows. By removing it, we instruct Cypher to collect everything together. This is quite different from SQL, where you have to explicitly specify grouping keys and return values. Cypher is more concise and I find it more intuitive than SQL.

# Conditional expressions

Consider this scenario: we want to write a query that computes the average scores of books in the following two categories:

- **Recent books**: This category contains all books published in the year 2010 or later

- **Other books**: This category contains all other books published before 2010 or without a date of publication

We already know how to compute the average of a value in a group based on a property value, but here we have an arbitrary grouping based on a condition. We can use the CASE WHEN expression to express this condition. The query will be as follows:

```
MATCH (b:Book)<-[r:Votes]-(:User)
OPTIONAL MATCH (b) -[p:PublishedBy]-> (c)
RETURN
  CASE WHEN p.year >= 2010 THEN 'Recent'
    ELSE 'Old' END as category,
  AVG(r.score)
```

In this query, we introduced a CASE WHEN expression in the RETURN clause. The expression evaluates to the Recent string if the year of publication is 2010 or later, and Old if otherwise. In the RETURN clause, we have the book category that results from the CASE WHEN expression and AVG(r.score); therefore, Cypher will group the score average by the book category. In fact, the result is as follows:

```
+-----------------------------+
| category | AVG(r.score)     |
+-----------------------------+
| "Recent" | 4.4333333333333333 |
| "Old"    | 4.9767123287671234 |
+-----------------------------+
```

There are two types of CASE WHEN expressions. The type we have just learned is the generic one. It is used when we have a set of alternative conditions to verify. If we just have a set of possible values, then we can use the simple form. Here is an example:

```
MATCH (b:Book)<-[r:Votes]-(:User)
OPTIONAL MATCH (b) -[p:PublishedBy]-> (c)
RETURN
  CASE p.year % 2
    WHEN 0 THEN 'Even'
    WHEN 1 THEN 'Odd'
    ELSE 'Unknown' END as parity,
  AVG(r.score)
```

This query computes the score average grouped by the parity publication year. Here, the CASE WHEN statement is slightly different; we have an expression right after the CASE keyword. This expression is evaluated and compared to the values in the WHEN clauses. If one of them matches, the corresponding value expressed in the THEN clause is picked; otherwise, the ELSE value is returned. The result is as follows:

```
+----------------------------+
| parity | AVG(r.score)      |
+----------------------------+
| "Odd"  | 4.0               |
| "Even" | 3.4               |
| <null> | 4.4413793103448276 |
+----------------------------+
```

You may wonder why do we have a null value instead of Unknown in the result. The reason is that if p.year is a null value, the expression in the case cannot be evaluated. To make null values fall in our condition, we will again resort to the COALESCE function. The query is as follows:

```
MATCH (b:Book)<-[r:Votes]-(:User)
OPTIONAL MATCH (b) -[p:PublishedBy]-> (c)
RETURN
  CASE COALESCE(p.year % 2, -1)
    WHEN 0 THEN 'Even'
    WHEN 1 THEN 'Odd'
    ELSE 'Unknown' END as parity,
  AVG(r.score)
```

# Separating query parts using WITH

Suppose you want the books sorted by average score, with highest score at the top; for this, we can write the following query:

```
MATCH (b:Book) <-[r:Votes]- (:User)
RETURN b, AVG(r.score) as avgScore
ORDER BY avgScore DESC
```

This query returns all books that have votes with their average score. However, that could be a huge number of books, almost the entire database. Suppose you are looking only for books with a score greater than or equal to 4. Where would you place the WHERE clause? Of course, you can't put it before the RETURN clause because the average score is computed there. We have to split the query in two: a part to compute the averages and a part for filtering and sorting.

The WITH keyword exists for this reason. The query is as follows:

```
MATCH (b:Book) <-[r:Votes]- (:User)
WITH b, AVG(r.score) as avgScore
WHERE avgScore >=4
RETURN b, avgScore
ORDER BY avgScore DESC
```

The result is as follows:

```
+--------------------------------------------+
| b                                | avgScore |
+--------------------------------------------+
| Node[171]{title:"Anna Karenina"} | 4.4      |
| Node[141]{title:"Tales"}         | 4.0      |
+--------------------------------------------+
```

This example shows us how to re-use an existing query to perform further processing. We can perform the following tasks:

- Give an alias to computed values in the RETURN function
- Replace the RETURN keyword with the WITH keyword
- Append the new part to the previous using the variable declared in the WITH function

Splitting queries is useful to filter data, which is otherwise difficult. This is done by combining the WHERE function with the MATCH or OPTIONAL MATCH functions. For example, if we want the year of publication of the book with the best score, the following query can be used:

```
MATCH (b:Book) <-[r:Votes]- (:User)
WITH b, AVG(r.score) as avgScore
ORDER BY avgScore DESC
LIMIT 1
OPTIONAL MATCH (b) -[p:PublishedBy]-> ()
RETURN b.title, p.year
```

This query is understandable. In the first four lines, we are looking for the book with the best score. In the remaining part of the query, we get the year of publication.

# The UNION statement

Suppose we want to know how many books and how many authors are stored in our database. We can perform two queries to get these values, but with the UNION statement, we can merge these data together. Just put the UNION keyword between two or more queries, as shown in the following query:

```
MATCH (b:Book)
RETURN 'Books' as type, COUNT(b) as cnt
UNION ALL
MATCH (a:Person)
RETURN 'Authors' as type, COUNT(a) as cnt
```

The result is as follows:

```
+----------------+
| type      | cnt |
+----------------+
| "Books"   | 150 |
| "Authors" | 142 |
+----------------+
```

The only condition we must be careful of with the UNION statement is that the result set must have the same number of columns and the columns must have the same names.

You're perhaps wondering why we used the UNION ALL statement and not the UNION statement in the previous example. There is a subtle difference between them — the UNION statement removes duplicated rows after merging results, so it is slower.

> If you don't care about duplicated rows, or you already know that your result set has no duplicates, use the UNION ALL statement because it faster than the UNION statement.

# Summary

In this chapter, you learned some advanced techniques to query a Neo4j database. First of all, we used the WHERE statement to filter data. Text values can be filtered using regular expressions, which are very flexible and powerful tools to work with strings. Numbers can be filtered using mathematical operators and functions. Logical expressions can be built using Boolean operators (OR, AND, XOR, and NOT). Collections can be filtered using collection predicates.

Paging data is an important feature for a database, especially when it can be very large. You learned how to page data using the LIMIT and SKIP keywords. An important part of this chapter is about aggregating. You learned how to use the RETURN clause to aggregate data with the most common aggregation functions, especially COUNT, SUM, AVG, MAX, and MIN. Finally, we took a look at two useful features of this language: the WITH and UNION keywords. The WITH keyword is used to split queries in order to make them easier to write. The UNION keyword is used to merge two or more result sets.

In the next chapter, you will learn how to create a database using Cypher writing clauses.

# 3
# Manipulating the Database

In the previous chapters, you learned how to query and work with data stored in a database. Yet, you don't know how to modify the database because, as you are going to see, the processes of creating, updating, and deleting data are topics strictly related to all the notions we have learned so far. In this chapter, we will learn the following:

- How to use Neo4j Browser to prototype and test your queries quickly
- The syntax and usage of the CREATE clause
- How to merge data with an existing database
- How to delete data from a database

## Using Neo4j Browser

Neo4j Browser is a very useful tool that is distributed with Neo4j. It's a web-based shell client, which we can use to interact in real time with a Neo4j Server database without configuring or programming anything other than Cypher. Here, no Java code is needed. The purpose of Neo4j Browser is to provide an easy interface for prototyping databases and testing queries. It can be accessed by following these steps:

1. Start Neo4j Community. You can download the latest version from the Neo4j download page at http://www.neo4j.org/download.
2. Choose a database location path and click on the **Start** button.

3.  Wait a few seconds while the database is created.

4.  Click on the link that appears in the **Status** panel (for example,
    `http://localhost:7474/`) to open Neo4j Browser.

Now you should see your preferred browser open the web page as shown in the
following screenshot:

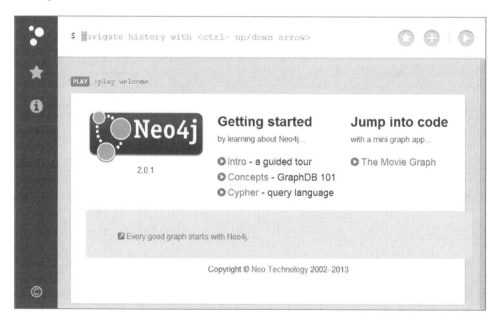

At the top of the page, there is the shell prompt. Here, you can write the Cypher queries you want to be executed in real time against the database. The results will be shown as output in the panel below. For example, let's take a look at the content of the database by writing the following query:

```
MATCH (n) RETURN n
```

The panel below shifts and shows the query result. On the right-hand side of the result panel, we have two buttons: one that shows the graph visualization and one that shows the grid visualization:

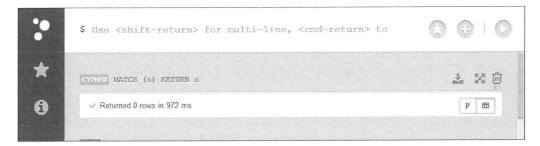

As we saw in the first chapter, Neo4j Server supports a **REST API**. So, if you're going to use a Neo4j database server, you'll use a REST API to interact with it. If you're going to interact with the database server using a programming language that is supported by a driver of your choice, note that this driver (whether PHP, C#, Python, or any other) will wrap REST calls to the Neo4j REST API. Although the REST API is not strictly necessary if you aren't a driver developer, it can be really useful to know that Neo4j Browser can also be used to test REST API calls when something goes wrong with the driver. A REST API is a layer that runs on a database server that actually performs queries/modifications on databases. Java, C#, and other drivers just abstract calls to this API, allowing programmers to write their applications without worrying about the stack and the protocol used to communicate with the database.

For example, you can send the previous query to Neo4j with REST by typing the following code in the prompt:

```
:POST /db/data/cypher { "query": "MATCH (n) RETURN n" }
```

Neo4j Browser returns the following result:

```
{
  "columns": [
    "n"
  ],
  "data": []
}
```

The database is empty so we get zero rows. It's time to fill the database with new nodes and relationships.

# Creating nodes and relationships

In this section, we will learn how to create nodes and relationships in our database. Let's start with the simplest example, that is, creating our first node. In the prompt, just type the following:

```
CREATE ()
```

This command creates a node without properties or labels. It's equivalent to the following Java code:

```
Node n = graphDb.createNode();
```

The result panel now shows the result as **Created 1 node, returned 0 rows in 825 ms**.

The preceding command returned zero rows because we had no RETURN clause. It just created an anonymous node in the database. This node is not very useful as it is, as it can be referenced only by an ID. However, the command lets us introduce the CREATE clause. The CREATE clause takes one argument: the pattern that expresses the nodes and relationships to be created. All the patterns we learned in *Chapter 1, Querying Neo4j Effectively with Pattern Matching*, are supported here. Any variable used in the expression is bounded to the newly created object so that it can be used further in the query. For example, consider the following query:

```
CREATE (n)
RETURN n
```

By adding the RETURN clause, we get a result that consists of one row: the node that was created earlier. Well, let's have a look at the CREATE clause in action with common tasks.

## Labels and properties

In this chapter, we'll model a social network. A user registered in the social network is a node. Let's create a new one using the following query:

```
CREATE (u:User)
RETURN u
```

If you switch to the tabular view, Neo4j Browser's reply will be **Added 1 label, created 1 node, returned 1 row in 155 ms**. This reply can be described as follows:

- The added label is User, which is added to the new node.
- The created node is bounded to the variable *u*.
- The variable *u* is returned to us. The graphical visualizer in the result panel shows us a chart, as shown in the following screenshot:

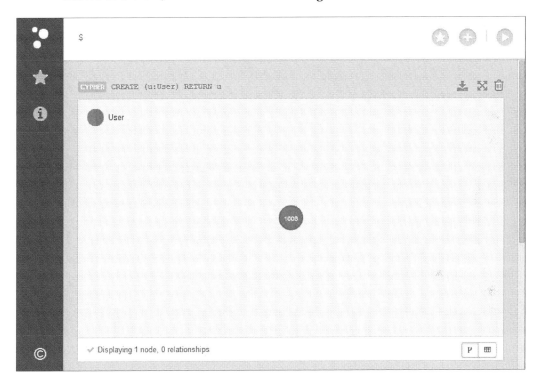

The number inside the node is the node ID assigned by Neo4j. You will most likely get another value when you run the previous query in your database.

## Multiple labels

You can add as many labels as you need to a node by chaining them in a single definition. The following query creates another user with two labels, User and Inactive:

```
CREATE (u:User:Inactive)
RETURN u
```

The result is a new node.

# Properties

The nodes we have created so far have no properties. The CREATE clause supports the creation of properties along with their nodes in a unique query. To do so, just apply the patterns we introduced in *Chapter 1, Querying Neo4j Effectively with Pattern Matching*, as shown in the following query:

```
CREATE (u:User {name: "John", surname: "Doe"})
RETURN u
```

If you copy and paste the preceding query in the prompt, you will see the result panel showing a single node. When you click on the node, a window appears, showing the properties of the node.

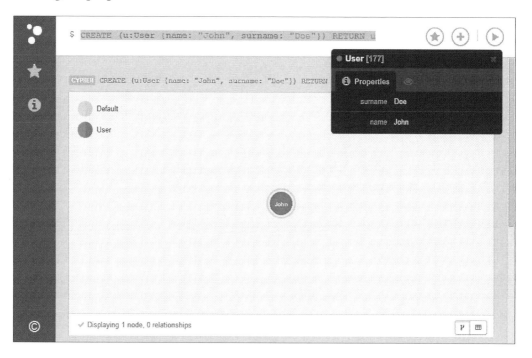

If you look at the preceding screenshot, you will see that the node in the middle shows its name as the property value instead of its ID. The property value shown in the node can be set using the style tab, which can be opened by clicking on the node itself. This setting is just for visualization; it doesn't affect your database.

# Creating multiple patterns

By separating patterns with a comma, you get them to be treated separately resulting into the creation of multiple patterns. The following query creates three users in a single call:

```
CREATE (a:User {name: "Jane", surname: "Roe"}),
       (b:User {name: "Carlos", surname: "Garcia"}),
       (c:User {name: "Mei", surname: "Weng"})
```

No result is returned, since the RETURN clause is missing. If we add RETURN a,b,c to the query, we will get three nodes in a single row, one per column. To get them in a single column, add RETURN [a,b,c] at the end of the query. Note that you won't see any effect in the graph visualization panel of Neo4j Browser, but the return values are shown in a tabular view; clearly, they are crucial if you query the database programmatically.

# Creating relationships

If you want to create relationships along with nodes, it is easy; just use the relationship pattern, as shown in the following query:

```
CREATE (:User {name: "Jack", surname: "Smith"})
       -[:Sibling]->
       (:User {name: "Mary", surname: "Smith"})
```

Neo4j Browser shows a log of all the operations that are executed. The result shown is **Added 2 labels, created 2 nodes, set 4 properties, created 1 relationship, returned 0 rows in 472 ms**.

The previous example gives us the opportunity to discuss about the direction of a relationship. In Neo4j, every relationship is directed, so you must specify a direction once it is created. However, as the paths between nodes can be traversed in both directions, the application has the responsibility to either ignore or consider the direction of the querying path. In fact, as mentioned in *Chapter 1, Querying Neo4j Effectively with Pattern Matching*, you can query a relation and ignore the direction. The following query is an example of this:

```
MATCH (a) -[r:Sibling]-(b)
RETURN a,r,b
```

Note that ignoring the direction of queries has performance implications on large datasets, especially if used in conjunction with variable length paths. We will see this in detail in the next chapter.

# Creating full paths

Using a path pattern, you can create a full path in Neo4j. The following query illustrates how this is done:

```
CREATE p = (jr:User {name: "Jack", surname: "Roe"})
          -[:Sibling]->
                (:User {name: "Mary", surname: "Roe"})
          -[:Friend]->
                (:User {name: "Jane", surname: "Jones"})
          -[:Coworker {company: "Acme Inc."}]
                ->(jr)
RETURN p
```

The preceding query creates three nodes and then three relationships among them: Sibling, Friend, and Coworker. The latter has the company name as its property, and the end node is the first node of the path (the user Jack Roe). Look at the way we have referenced a node that was specified previously by putting a variable in the node's definition (jr:User {name: "Jack", surname: "Roe"}) and using the variable jr afterwards.

As the query returns the path, Neo4j Browser shows a graph of the whole path, as shown in the following screenshot:

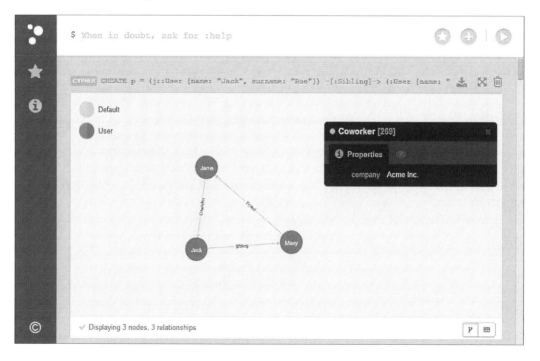

## Creating relationships between existing nodes using read-and-write queries

You can use the CREATE clause in conjunction with the MATCH statement to add relationships between existing nodes. For example, the following query creates a relationship between two nodes:

```
MATCH (a:User {name: "Jack", surname: "Roe"}),
      (b:User {name: "Jack", surname: "Smith"})
CREATE (a) -[r:Knows]-> (b)
RETURN a,r,b
```

The MATCH statement matches the user nodes Jack Roe and Jack Smith with the variables a and b; then, the CREATE clause creates a relation of the type Knows between them. Finally, both the user nodes and their new relationship are returned as output.

Generally, this kind of read-and-write query has the following two parts:

- The first is the reading part. Here, we can use any reading function (START, MATCH, OPTIONAL MATCH, and WITH).

- The second part is writing, where we can use the CREATE command or other writing clauses that we are going to learn in the next section.

# Modifying existing data

The last query in the previous section creates a relationship between two nodes. If we run that query twice, we will have two relations between those nodes. In most cases, this redundancy is unnecessary and useless for us. Suppose our social network was online and had a button called "Add Friend". In this scenario, if two users, say A and B, click on this button at the same time to add each other as friends, the relation would be doubled in the database. This is a waste of storage. In this context, we need to check the database and create the relation only if it does not exist. This is why an OPTIONAL MATCH clause is required to prevent double storage. This is illustrated in the following query:

```
MATCH (a:User {name: "Jack", surname: "Roe"}),
      (b:User {name: "Jack", surname: "Smith"})
OPTIONAL MATCH (a) -[r:Knows]- (b)
WITH a,r,b
WHERE r IS NULL
CREATE (a) -[rn:Knows]-> (b)
RETURN a,rn,b
```

This query, first of all, finds the users Jack Roe and Jack Smith in the database (the MATCH clause), then checks whether they are connected through a relation of the type Knows (the OPTIONAL MATCH clause). If not, (r IS NULL means that the relation cannot be found) the CREATE command that follows will create a relationship between the nodes. The WITH clause is necessary to apply the WHERE clause to the whole query. If the WITH clause is not used, the WHERE clause is applied only to the OPTIONAL MATCH clause.

If you run the preceding query after the query mentioned in the *Creating relationships between existing nodes using read-and-write queries* section, you'll get no rows. This is because the relationship is already created in the database. Clearly, this query isn't easy to read or write and it's error-prone. For these reasons, Cypher provides us with two keywords to deal with existing data.

# Creating unique patterns

The complexity of the preceding query is due to the fact that we have to check the nonexistence of a relationship before creating it. This is because we want that relationship to be unique. Fortunately, Cypher provides us with a command that wraps such a check and ensures that the pattern specified is unique in the database.

For example, we can rewrite the preceding query using the CREATE UNIQUE command, as shown in the following query:

```
MATCH (a:User {name: "Jack", surname: "Roe"}),
      (b:User {name: "Jack", surname: "Smith"})
CREATE UNIQUE (a) -[rn:Knows]-> (b)
RETURN a,rn,b
```

Using the CREATE UNIQUE command in the preceding query saved us from writing the entire OPTIONAL MATCH and WHERE clauses. My preferred motto is that the more code you write, the more bugs you hide; here, the latter is the preferred choice.

However there are two important differences between the the preceding query and the one in the previous section. They are as follows:

- If the CREATE UNIQUE command finds the relationship multiple times in the database, it will throw an error. For example, if two instances of the Knows relationship exist between the users Jack Roe and Jack Smith, then the query with the CREATE UNIQUE command will fail with an error, while the query with the OPTIONAL MATCH command will succeed (it will not create the relationship). Anyway, both the CREATE UNIQUE and the OPTIONAL MATCH commands won't make any modifications to the database. This difference is not a disadvantage of the CREATE UNIQUE command, rather an advantage. An error thrown by the query means that the database is corrupted as it has multiple instances of a relationship (or any pattern) that should be unique.

In the next chapter, we will learn how to enforce certain assertions using constraints.

- The query with the OPTIONAL MATCH command returns a row only if it creates a new relationship. However, the query with the CREATE UNIQUE command will return a result if it finds a relationship or creates a new one. This can be a useful feature in some contexts; we can know the state of certain paths in the database after the CREATE UNIQUE command is executed without performing another read-only query.

Yet, the CREATE UNIQUE command can be even more useful. Suppose we don't know if a user named Jack Smith has been created; if not we have to create and link it to the user Jack Roe. Consider the following read-and-write query:

```
MATCH (a:User {name: "Jack", surname: "Roe"})
CREATE UNIQUE (a) -[rn:Knows]->
                  (b:User {name: "Jack", surname: "Smith"})
RETURN a,rn,b
```

First of all, it looks for the user Jack Roe in the database, binding it to the variable a. If it cannot be found, the query will finish the execution and return zero rows. Otherwise, it executes the CREATE UNIQUE command, and there are four possible scenarios, which are listed as follows:

1. The full path already exists and it is unique; we have the user node Jack Roe with exactly one relationship with the user node Jack Smith. In this case, the existing nodes are bound to the variables a, rn, and b. Then, these variables are returned as result.

2. Neither the Jack Smith node nor the relationship exists in the database. In this case, the CREATE UNIQUE command creates the full path. The new relation is bound to the variable rn, while the new node is bound to the variable b.

3. When there are multiple paths, the path `(a)-[:Knows]-(b)` exists multiple times. For example, the `Knows` relationship exists multiple times between the nodes. If this happens, a **Neo.ClientError.Statement.ConstraintViolation** error is thrown because the `CREATE UNIQUE` command can't deal with multiple patterns.

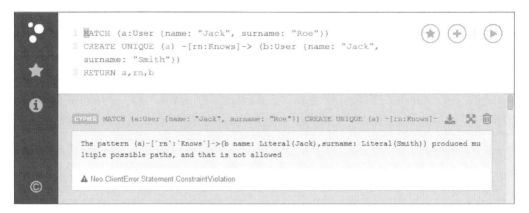

```
1 MATCH (a:User {name: "Jack", surname: "Roe"})
2 CREATE UNIQUE (a) -[rn:Knows]-> (b:User {name: "Jack",
  surname: "Smith"})
3 RETURN a,rn,b
```

```
CYPHER MATCH (a:User {name: "Jack", surname: "Roe"}) CREATE UNIQUE (a) -[rn:Knows]-

The pattern (a)-[`rn`:`Knows`]->(b name: Literal(Jack),surname: Literal(Smith)) produced mu
ltiple possible paths, and that is not allowed

⚠ Neo.ClientError.Statement.ConstraintViolation
```

4. Both `Jack Roe` and `Jack Smith` exist in the database as nodes, but there is no `Knows` relationship between them. As the matching follows the all-or-none rule, the Cypher engine creates a new `Jack Smith` node and a new relationship bound to the variable `rn`. This is due to the fact that the purpose of the `CREATE UNIQUE` command is to ensure that a whole pattern is unique in the graph and if the node already exists but not the relationship, we do not have the whole pattern in the graph.

The last scenario could be a problem because we would have duplicated a user in the database. We can resolve this issue using the `MERGE` clause, which is discussed later in the chapter.

To summarize, the following diagram shows how the CREATE UNIQUE clause works:

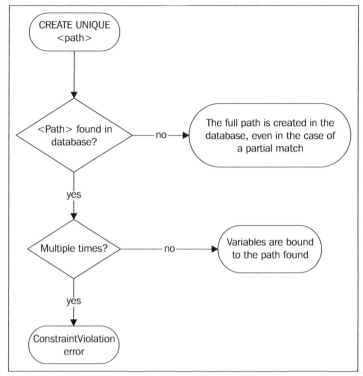

## Complex patterns

Just as the MATCH and the CREATE clauses, you can join simple patterns to describe a complex one. Consider the following query:

```
MATCH (a:User {name: "Jack", surname: "Roe"})
CREATE UNIQUE (a) -[kn:Knows]->
                   (b:User {name: "Jack", surname: "Smith"}),
              (a) -[cw:Colleague]-> (b)
```

This query creates two relationships between two users. Only the relationships not found in the database are created. If you launch this query after the query from the previous section, you'll get a the message **Created 1 relationship, returned 0 rows in 307 ms**.

In fact, the relationship `Knows` and the user `Jack Smith` were already in the database, while the `Colleague` relationship was missing. If all of them exist, this query makes no modifications to the graph. The second time you launch this query, you'll get the result **Returned 0 rows in 229 ms**, which means that neither relationships nor nodes were created.

Note that the `CREATE UNIQUE` command looks for a path that exactly matches the pattern. So, for example, the following query won't match either the existing user node or the existing relationship. Instead, it will create a new relationship and a new node.

```
MATCH (a:User {name: "Jack", surname: "Roe"})
CREATE UNIQUE (a) -[rn:Knows {friend: true}]->
    (b:User {name: "Jack",surname: "Smith", age:34})
```

In fact, we haven't set the `age` property to the user `Jack Smith` in our database. However, this could return weird results in some cases (as the preceding example). How to update the user node without creating a new user if a new property is found in the pattern? Again, this issue can be solved using the `MERGE` clause.

# Setting properties and labels

First of all, we need to know how to set the property of an existing node. The `SET` clause is just the ticket. Let's start with an example. Consider the following query:

```
MATCH (a:User {name: "Jack", surname: "Roe"})
SET a.age = 34
RETURN a
```

This query takes the user node `Jack Roe` and sets the `age` property for it; then, it returns the updated node. Neo4j Browser shows the result as **Set 1 property, returned 1 row in 478 ms**.

Note that the `SET` clause here works on the nodes found using the `MATCH` clause. This means that we can set a property on a huge list of nodes if we don't write the `MATCH` clause carefully. The following query sets the `city` property on all the nodes with the surname property `Roe`:

```
MATCH (a:User {surname: "Roe"})
SET a.place = "London"
RETURN a
```

In our database, this query updates three nodes: `Jane`, `Jack`, and `Mary Roe`. Neo4j Browser shows the result as **Set 3 properties, returned 3 rows in 85 ms**.

Again, you can change several assignment expressions to make more property changes at the same time. For example, to set the country as well, the query will be as follows:

```
MATCH (a:User {surname: "Roe"})
SET a.place="London", a.country="UK"
RETURN a
```

The syntax to set a property to a relationship is the same, as shown in the following query:

```
MATCH (:User{surname: "Roe"})-[r:Knows]-()
SET r.friend = true
```

This query finds all the `Knows` relationships of users with the surname property `Roe` and sets the property `friend` to `true` for all of them.

## Cloning a node

The `SET` clause can also be used to copy all the properties of a node to another. For example, to copy the node x to the node y, use the following query:

```
SET y = x
```

Note that all of the destination node's properties will be removed before the node is copied.

Copying a node is useful when a node needs cloning. For example, in our social network, there could be a function to create an alias identity; the user could start cloning his/her own identity and then modify the new one. This command can be coded as shown in the following query:

```
MATCH (a:User {name: "Jack", surname: "Roe"})
CREATE (b:Alias)-[:AliasOf]->(a)
WITH a,b
SET b = a
RETURN a,b
```

This query, once it finds the user node to clone, creates a new node with labels `Alias` and `User` and have a relationship with the source node of the type `AliasOf`. Then, it copies all the properties from the source node to it and finally returns the node. The command `SET b = a` doesn't affect the labels of the node b or its relationships; it just copies the properties.

## Adding labels to nodes

The SET clause can also be used to add one or more labels to a node, as shown in the following query:

```
MERGE (b:User {name: "Jack", surname: "Smith"})
SET b:Inactive
```

The only difference is that we need to use the label separator instead of the property assignment. To chain more labels, just append them with the separator, as shown in the following query:

```
MERGE (b:User {name: "Jack", surname: "Smith"})
SET b:Inactive:NewUser:MustConfirmEmail
```

# Merging matched patterns

The MERGE clause is a new feature of Cypher, introduced by Neo4j 2.0. The features of the MERGE clause are similar to those of the CREATE UNIQUE command. It checks whether a pattern exists in the graph. If not, it creates the whole pattern; otherwise, it matches it. The main difference is that the pattern doesn't have to be unique. The other differences are as follows:

- The MERGE clause supports the single node pattern
- The MERGE clause allows users to specify what to do when the pattern is matched and what to do when the pattern is being created

In an earlier section, we saw two issues with the CREATE UNIQUE command. They are as follows:

1. How to create a new node if the pattern does not match, but match the existing node if the node exists?

2. How to set the variables when merging nodes and relationships?

To answer the first question, let's recall the second query from the *Creating unique patterns* section:

```
MATCH (a:User {name: "Jack", surname: "Roe"})
CREATE UNIQUE (a) -[rn:Knows]->
                  (b:User {name: "Jack", surname: "Smith"})
```

Now, if the intent of this query is to match an existing `Jack Smith` user node before creating a relationship to it, it will fail. This is because if the relationship does not exist, a new `Jack Smith` node will be created again. We can take advantage of the single node pattern supported by the MERGE clause and write the following query:

```
MATCH (a:User {name: "Jack", surname: "Roe"})
MERGE (b:User {name: "Jack", surname: "Smith"})
WITH a,b
MERGE (a) -[rn:Knows]-> (b)
RETURN a,rn,b
```

To accomplish our goal, we had to split the query in two parts using the WITH clause. The first step is to find the `Jack Roe` user node in the graph with the MATCH clause. Then, the first MERGE clause ensures that a node with exactly two properties—the name `Jack` and surname `Smith`—exists in the database. In the latter part of the query, the focus is on the relationship `Knows` between the two nodes involved; the second MERGE clause ensures that the relationship exists after the execution. What happens if the `Jack Smith` user exists twice in the database and the nodes are already related? The MERGE clause wouldn't fail; it would succeed, returning two rows.

 In the next chapter, we will learn how to create constraints in the database to ensure that it won't ever create nodes with the same property value.

Now, about the second problem of how to set properties during merging operations, the MERGE clause supports two interesting features. They are as follows:

- ON MATCH SET: This clause is used to set one or more properties or labels on the matched nodes
- ON CREATE SET: This clause is used to set one or more properties or labels on the new nodes

For example, suppose that we want to set the `Jack Smith` user node's `place` property to `London` only if we are creating it, then the following query can be used:

```
MERGE (b:User {name: "Jack", surname: "Smith"})
ON CREATE SET b.place = "London"
```

If at the same time, we want to set his `age` property to `34` only if the user already exists, then the following query can be used:

```
MERGE (b:User {name: "Jack", surname: "Smith"})
ON CREATE SET b.place = "London"
ON MATCH SET b.age = 34
```

Clearly, when we want to set a property in both cases, you can just append a SET clause to a MERGE clause, as shown in the following query:

```
MERGE (b:User {name: "Jack", surname: "Smith"})
SET b.age = 34
```

 Once you learn how to use the MERGE clause and the CREATE UNIQUE command, you may wonder when to use either of these. As a general rule, when in doubt, you should use the CREATE UNIQUE command when the pattern is conceived as a whole path that must be unique in the graph.

## Idempotent queries

In certain applications, such as websites with several client types, parallel applications, and so on, some commands happen to be sent multiple times from external layers to the backend. This is due to a number of reasons, for example, user interfaces are not up to date, users can send a command multiple times, synchronization issues, and so on. In these cases, you could get the command to be executed multiple times; clearly you don't want the second or the *nth* execution to have an effect on the database. Commands that are executed once but have no effect when executed multiple times again on the same graph later are idempotent. Both MERGE and SET clauses allow you to write idempotent commands that nowadays are very useful in these growing contexts.

# Deleting data

Cypher provides two clauses to delete data. They are as follows:

- REMOVE: This clause is used to remove labels and properties from nodes or relationships
- DELETE: This clause is used to delete nodes and relationships from the database

# Removing labels

To remove a label from a node, you must use the REMOVE clause. The syntax is similar to the one for the SET clause, as shown in the following query:

```
MERGE (b:User {name: "Jack", surname: "Smith"})
REMOVE b:Inactive:MustConfirmEmail
```

This query removes the labels `Inactive` and `MustConfirmEmail` from the node that was matched. Note that we have chained the labels using the colon separator. If the node already doesn't have one or all of the labels specified, this query will not fail; it will only remove the labels it can remove.

# Removing properties

The `REMOVE` clause is the opposite of the `SET` clause. It can be used to remove a property from a node, as shown in the following query:

```
MERGE (b:User {name: "Jack", surname: "Smith"})
REMOVE b.age
```

Anyway, as Neo4j does not store `NULL` properties, the same result can be achieved by setting the property to `NULL`, as shown in the following query:

```
MERGE (b:User {name: "Jack", surname: "Smith"})
SET b.age = NULL
```

The preceding query can be used effectively when working with parameters. In fact, you can write the query as following:

```
MERGE (b:User {name: {name}, surname: {surname}})
SET b.age = {age}
```

This query can be used to both set the `age` property of a user and remove the `age` parameter from the node. Again, all operations with the `REMOVE` and `SET` clauses are idempotent, so you don't need to worry if the properties exist before you remove them.

# Deleting nodes and relations

If you want to delete a node, use the `DELETE` clause, as shown in the following query:

```
MATCH (c:User {name: "Mei", surname: "Weng"})
DELETE c
```

This query looks for a node with the given name and surname using the `MATCH` clause and then tries to delete it.

Three important points about the preceding query are as follows:

- It is idempotent. If no node is found, the query won't fail; it just won't delete anything.
- Properties are deleted with the node. You do not need to remove all the properties before deleting the node.

- On the other hand, if the node to delete has at least one relationship with another node, the query will fail and raise an exception, which can be seen in the following screenshot:

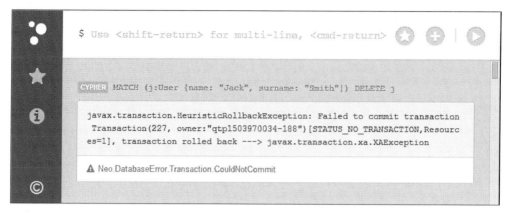

```
$ Use <shift-return> for multi-line, <cmd-return>

CYPHER  MATCH (j:User {name: "Jack", surname: "Smith"}) DELETE j

javax.transaction.HeuristicRollbackException: Failed to commit transaction
  Transaction(227, owner:"qtp1503970034-188")[STATUS_NO_TRANSACTION,Resourc
  es=1], transaction rolled back ---> javax.transaction.xa.XAException

⚠ Neo.DatabaseError.Transaction.CouldNotCommit
```

Therefore, before deleting a node, you must be sure that it is not involved in any relationship. If it is, then how to delete a relationship? The syntax is the same; you just have to use the right variable, as shown in the following query:

```
MATCH (:User {name: "Mei", surname: "Weng"}) -[r]- ()
DELETE r
```

This query deletes any relationship that involves the user that was matched. So, to delete a node along with all its relationships, should we perform two queries? Not at all, we just need the following query:

```
MATCH (c:User {name: "Jack", surname: "Smith"})
OPTIONAL MATCH (c)-[r]- ()
DELETE r, c
```

This query deletes the node and any of its relationships. It, first of all, finds the node, then it matches it with any existing relationship. The OPTIONAL MATCH clause is needed because if we use a simple MATCH clause, the query won't delete a node with zero relations. Finally, the DELETE clause causes the relations and the node to be deleted.

# Clearing the whole database

Generalizing the preceding query, we can clear the whole database, deleting all the nodes and relationships, just by changing the first MATCH clause to take all user nodes as argument, as shown in the following query:

```
MATCH (a)
OPTIONAL MATCH (a)-[r]-()
DELETE a, r
```

We can also do this by using the START clause on all the nodes. We get the same result. The query is as follows:

```
START a = node(*)
OPTIONAL MATCH (a)-[r]-()
DELETE a, r
```

Use it carefully because it will delete all of the data from the graph.

# Loops

Due to the nature of the Cypher queries, usually, you won't need something like a loop used in other programming languages. In fact, as you have probably already realized, the general structure of a Cypher query is formed by three phases and each one of these is optional. The phases are as follows:

- **Read**: This is the phase where you read data from the graph using the START, MATCH, or OPTIONAL MATCH clauses.

- **Write**: This is the phase where you modify the graph using CREATE, MERGE, SET, and all the other clauses we learned in this chapter.

- **Return**: This is the phase where you choose what to return to the caller by using the RETURN clause. This part can be replaced by a WITH clause and then the query can start again from the read phase.

The read phase is important because the write phase will be executed for every item found in the read phase. For example, consider the following query:

```
MATCH (a:User {surname: "Roe"})
SET a.place = "London"
RETURN a
```

In this query, the SET command will be executed once for each node found with the MATCH clause. Consequently, you usually won't need an explicit for-loop statement.

# Working with collections

The unique case when you need to iterate is when you work with collections. In the previous chapter, we saw that Cypher can use different kinds of collections: collections of nodes, relationships, and properties. Sometimes, you may need to iterate on a collection and perform some write operation consequently. There is a clause for this purpose, and it is the FOREACH clause. Its syntax is akin to the syntax of collection clauses we learned in the previous chapters. The syntax is as follows:

```
FOREACH (variable IN collection | command)
```

Let's see it in action with an example. Suppose that in our social network, you want a function that traverses the shortest path from one user to another and creates a new relationship of the type MaybeKnows between each node visited and the first user. Does it sound difficult to achieve this with a single query? No, it can be done with just two clauses: a MATCH clause and a FOREACH clause, as shown in the following query:

```
MATCH p=shortestPath(
    (a:User {name: "Mary", surname: "Smith"})-[*]-
        (b:User {name: "Jane", surname: "Jones"}) )
FOREACH (n IN tail(nodes(p)) |
    CREATE UNIQUE (n)-[:MaybeKnows]->(a))
```

In the first step, this query computes the shortest path between the two nodes, using the pattern we learned in *Chapter 1, Querying Neo4j Effectively with Pattern Matching*. Then, there is an iteration over all the nodes, except for the first node; for each node, a unique relation is created between the first node of the path (Mary Smith) and itself. Now, let's take a look at the content of the FOREACH clause, that is, tail(nodes(p)). The function nodes extracts all the nodes of the path, while the tail function returns all the items except for the first of a collection. In this case, we use the tail function because we don't want Cypher to create a relation between the user node Mary Smith and itself. In fact, Neo4j allows you to create self-loops. Self-loops are relations between a node and itself. Note that using self-loops is perfectly right in some contexts but not in this case. So, we have avoided it by using the tail function.

# Summary

In this chapter, you learned how to use Neo4j Browser. Thanks to this very useful testing and prototyping tool provided by Neo4j, you have learned a lot of new clauses needed to modify the graph, such as CREATE, CREATE UNIQUE, SET, MERGE, REMOVE, and DELETE.

Finally, you learned how to use the FOREACH clause to traverse a collection to perform write operations.

In the next chapter, we will examine in depth how to improve the performance of our Cypher queries, and how to enforce important assertions about our graph according to the peculiarities of the domain model.

# 4

# Improving Performance

Using Neo4j has several advantages, including a very natural model that allows you to easily express complex schemas with a lot of relations as well as **Atomicity**, **Consistency**, **Isolation**, and **Durability (ACID)** transactions. It gives a great performance compared to relational databases.

Performance is a key feature in some scenarios and drives developers and architects to choose Neo4j. In this chapter, you will learn about:

- Several performance issues that you face while using Cypher and some possible solutions

- How to profile a Cypher query to estimate its computational cost and its cost in terms of number of times I/O is accessed

- How to use the schema to preserve the integrity of the database and take advantage of it to improve performance

## Performance issues

We will focus on two common types of performance issues we face with Cypher. They are as follows:

- A long and complex query is executed too slow. The query can be a complex read-write query or a read-only query with aggregation, complex computations, and sorting.

- A small query is repeated many times, for example, in a loop cycle. The query itself does not underperform, but repeating it many times causes the whole operation to take a long time to finish.

Now, suppose that we have a huge database with a lot of nodes; for example, a database for a social network. In fact, if we are experiencing performance problems with small databases, we probably need to check the hardware, or the operating system, or the configuration of Neo4j because it's unusual to experience a very slow query with small datasets. In this chapter, we will see some configuration options of Neo4j that are useful when tuning the performance of the database.

To simulate performance issues, the example used in this chapter must have a lot of data. To fill our example database, we can create a number of nodes, with Neo4j Embedded, by writing some lines of the Java code in a loop. This is described in the following query:

```java
for (int i = 0; i < 1000; i++) {
  try (Transaction tx = graphDb.beginTx()) {
    Node node = graphDb.createNode();
    node.setProperty("email", "user" + i + "@learningcypher.com");
    node.setProperty("userId", i);
    node.addLabel(DynamicLabel.label("User"));

    if(i % 100 == 0)
      node.addLabel(DynamicLabel.label("Inactive"));

    tx.success();
  }
}
```

Each cycle, which is repeated 1000 times, creates a node, sets two properties (email and userId), and sets a label (User) to the node. The DynamicLabel.label("User") call allows us to specify a label without having to declare a statically-typed label implementation. Finally, after every 100 nodes, one node is set the Inactive label. Each step is executed in a transaction; this is a requirement as we are accessing the database. The problem here is that we have a lot of tiny transactions; every time we commit a transaction, Neo4j will access the disk to persist the data, leading to a performance overhead.

Alternatively, using any script language, you can generate a long Cypher query that joins a number of nodes to create then copy and paste the query in Neo4j Browser's prompt. This is described in the following query:

```
CREATE (:User {email: 'user0@learningcypher.com', userId: 0 }),
       (:User {email: 'user1@learningcypher.com', userId: 1 }),
       (:User {email: 'user2@learningcypher.com', userId: 2 }),
       (:User {email: 'user3@learningcypher.com', userId: 3 }),
```

The preceding query will create the same data in a single transaction. Neo4j will save the data in the memory and will persist everything simultaneously at the end. The problem here is that the Cypher engine must parse and process a huge string to translate it into a real operation that will be performed on the database. In the next sections, we will see the performance issues we have found in these two approaches in detail and how to get rid of them.

In the code bundle, which can be downloaded for free from the Packt Publishing website (http://www.packtpub.com/support), you will find the whole script generated there as well as the Java project with the Neo4j embedded example code. We'll see these in the rest of the chapter so that you can set up the database that is used as an example in this chapter.

From Neo4j 2.1 onwards, bulk creations can be performed by reading from a **comma-separated values** (CSV) file with the following new clause:

```
LOAD CSV FROM "file.csv"
CREATE (:User{email: csvLine[0], userId: csvLine[1] })
```

# Best practices and recommendations

You surely know the following famous quote from Donald Knuth, which is attributed to Tony Hoare:

> *"We should forget about small efficiencies, say about 97% of the time: premature optimization is the root of all evil. Yet we should not pass up our opportunities in that critical 3%."*

The sense of the quote is that you should avoid writing obfuscated, unreadable, and error-prone code in order to gain an insignificant performance advantage, because the most important performance gain will be achieved only in 3 percent of your code. However, you should take precautions to not lose the opportunity to improve performance in that critical percentage.

In this section, we will talk about those precautions; we will see some general rules to avoid well-known performance issues with Cypher. If you follow all of them, you will reduce the probability of facing poor performances in your applications without affecting the readability of your Cypher queries.

# Using parameterized queries

As you remember, in *Chapter 1, Querying Neo4j Effectively with Pattern Matching*, we introduced the usage of query parameters with Java. There we saw how query parameters can be useful to write readable and maintainable code. Yet, query parameters are a great ally to boost the performance of queries that are executed many times.

Consider, for example, the following simple query:

```
MATCH (n:User {email: 'user300@learningcypher.com'})
RETURN n
```

When you launch this query, the engine takes the query as a string literal. Now, it must parse the query, build an execution plan, and run it. An execution plan is a list of steps necessary to execute a query. In fact, as Cypher is a declarative language, when you write a query, you focus on results than on the operations needed to get them. However, this means that the Cypher engine must process the code and prepare a plan to achieve the result you want. Now, launch the same query with another e-mail ID, for example:

```
MATCH (n:User {email: 'user400@learningcypher.com'})
RETURN n
```

Then, the engine assumes that since the query is different, the plan could be different. So, the engine computes a new plan. However, this one will be the same as the previous query with only one difference: the e-mail ID of the user to be searched for.

Writing queries with parameters allows the engine to reuse the execution plan of a query because the engine can cache it. Instead, if you rewrite a new query multiple times, changing only some of the parameters each time, this period of time wasted becomes very important. If you are working with Neo4j embedded, you can use the parameters in a manner identical to the one explained in *Chapter 1, Querying Neo4j Effectively with Pattern Matching*. This is described in the following query:

```
import org.neo4j.cypher.javacompat.*;
import java.util.*;

ExecutionEngine engine = ...
Map<String,Object> params = new HashMap<>();
params.put("emailQuery", email);
ExecutionResult result = engine
    .execute("MATCH(n:User {email: {emailQuery}}) RETURN n",
            params);
```

You can estimate the performance gain of this code by launching it a number of times. In Java, one easy way to get the elapsed time is using the `System.nanoTime()` function. If you compare the time needed to run the previous query 2000 times with the time needed to run the same query without using parameters, you will have a result similar to the following on a common desktop machine:

```
MATCH(n:User {email: '" + email + "'}) RETURN n
duration: 11458.105746 ms
MATCH(n:User {email: {emailQuery}}) RETURN n
duration: 2014.814202 ms
```

The parameterized version is more than five times faster than the query with no parameters. It is more scalable as well. In fact, after running these queries 4000 times, you'll get a result that looks like the following:

```
MATCH(n:User {email: '" + email + "'}) RETURN n
duration: 20610.989327 ms
MATCH(n:User {email: {emailQuery}}) RETURN n
duration: 2450.090195 ms
```

Clearly, with the non-parameterized query, the time elapsed has almost doubled, while with the parameterized query, the time elapsed has raised only by 20 percent.

## Parameterized queries with the REST API

Parameterized queries are also supported by the REST API, and, by using them, you will get a performance gain. In fact, the server will cache the execution plans of your queries and won't need to parse each of them, just as we saw in the previous section with queries in Neo4j embedded.

To use parameters with the REST API, just mention the values along with the query in the `params` member of the JSON code posted to the server, as described in the following query:

```
{
  "query" : "MATCH (n {userId: {id}}) RETURN n.email",
  "params" : {
    "id" : 300
  }
}
```

The preceding query searches the e-mail ID of a user in the database. The user ID (`300`) is passed in a parameter.

As usual, you can test it using any REST client or in Neo4j Browser, prepending the following command to the JSON code you want to send:

```
:POST /db/data/cypher
```

The result can be seen in the following screenshot:

# Reusing ExecutionEngine

When you work with Neo4j Embedded, as execution plans of parameterized queries are cached by ExecutionEngine, it's crucial that you don't create a new engine for each query you launch. Rather, create one engine and use it as many times as possible.

You should avoid writing functions in the following manner:

```
public void dontWriteFunctionsLikeThis(String email) {
    ExecutionEngine engine = new
                   ExecutionEngine(graphDatabaseService);

    Map<String,Object> map = new HashMap<>();
    map.put("email", email);
    ExecutionResult result = engine
      .execute("MATCH(n:User {email: {email} }) RETURN n", map);
    // working with result
}
```

Instead, pass the engine in the constructor of the class and use it. This is described in the following query:

```
public class ReuseTheEngine {
    private final GraphDatabaseService graphDatabaseService;
    private final ExecutionEngine engine;

    public ReuseTheEngine(
            GraphDatabaseService graphDatabaseService,
            ExecutionEngine engine) {
        this.graphDatabaseService = graphDatabaseService;
        this.engine = engine;
    }

    public ResourceIterator<Node> find(String email) {
      Map<String,Object> map = new HashMap<>();
      map.put("email", email);
      ExecutionResult result = engine
        .execute("MATCH(n:User {email: {email} }) RETURN n", map);
    }
}
```

The class in the preceding code keeps the engine for the entire lifetime of the objects. It reuses the same engine every time the find method is invoked, ensuring that the engine caches execution plans.

Note that ExecutionEngine is thread safe, so you can create only one instance and share it among all the threads of your multithreaded applications as a singleton (otherwise, if you are using an inversion of control container, you can safely register the instance as a singleton in the container).

# Finding the optimum transaction size

When you start a transaction and execute several operations within it, Neo4j does not persist the changes in the database but keeps them in memory. Neo4j will persist the changes only once you commit the transaction. This means that the more operations you put in a single transaction, the more memory Neo4j must allocate to keep them. This results, first of all, in a progressive decay in performance, but it can even cause the server to go out of memory.

If you experience a performance decay while executing a long transaction, you can monitor the heap usage to figure out whether the problem resides in the heap usage or not. One useful, visual, and free tool that you can use is Java VisualVM. It is provided with any **Java Development Kit (JDK)**.

 If you only have console access to the server that is hosting Neo4j, you can use jvmtop (https://code.google.com/p/jvmtop/), an open source console application to monitor all **Java Virtual Machines (JVM)** that are running on the machine.

To start the tool, launch the following code from the command-line interface:

```
# jvisualvm
```

Once the tool starts, a list of applications running on the JVM can be seen on the left-hand side of the window. When you select an application, you will see a set of statistical data on the right-hand side.

In the preceding screenshot, let's consider only the **Memory** usage, deselecting **CPU**, **Classes**, and **Threads**. Did you note the peak marked with a vertical dotted line? You will get that when you launch a big transaction by creating 4000 nodes and setting 8000 properties and 4000 labels. The heap usage has jumped from about 30 MB to about 180 MB, but it's still an acceptable load in that machine. Yet, when analyzing the statistics, you get to know that the heap usage is too much for your machine and is affecting the performance of your application, you have the following two options:

- You can increase the heap size reserved for JVM. In Neo4j Server, under **Windows**, you can edit the `neo4j-community.vmoptions` file and, for example, add the following line of code to set the heap size to 4 GB:

  ```
  -Xmx4G
  ```

  In Linux or Neo4j Server for Windows, you can edit the `neo4j-wrapper.conf` file in the Neo4j configuration folder. You will have to add the following line of code:

  ```
  wrapper.java.initmemory=4096
  ```

  It is noteworthy that increasing the Java heap size is an operation that should be performed with caution—you should be aware of the services that are running on the machine and of the hardware limitation. Increasing the JVM heap size, in fact, will affect the other running services, depriving them of the heap memory needed to run. In addition, while the heap size becomes increasingly larger, the garbage collector will take greater amounts of time to clean the heap. So, despite having infinite RAM at your disposal, there is an empiric limit to the heap size that will give you an effective performance gain. If you exceed this limit, you will have a decay in performance instead.

- You can split the transaction into smaller ones. Whether to split it or not and how to split it depends on the business logic of your application. Anyway, it is noteworthy that if you split the transaction described previously into 40 smaller transactions, you'll get the graph shown in the following screenshot in the same machine. This time, the heap reserved is less than half of the one used before, although you have done the same operations. You have just split it into more transactions.

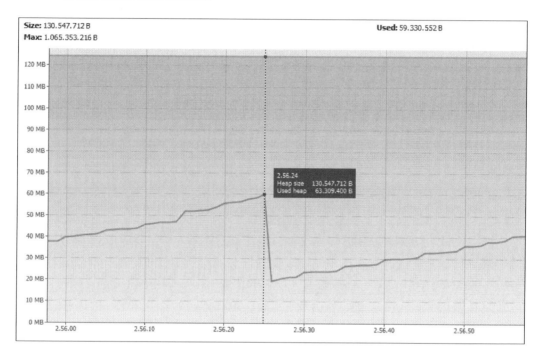

Above all this, as changes are persisted into the disk only when the transaction is committed, writing too many smaller transactions will cause as many I/O writes, causing performance deterioration due to the disk being accessed too many times. This effect can be alleviated by having many disks installed on the machine and configuring RAID 0 or RAID 5, but generally speaking, merging a lot of tiny transactions is a more scalable solution.

Note that the REST API provides two ways to merge many operations in only one transaction. The following are the two ways:

- The first one is by opening a transaction across multiple HTTP requests.

    1. To open a transaction, you have to post a payload to the /db/data/ transaction endpoint. An example payload could be the following:

    ```
    {
        "statements": [ {
            "statement": "CREATE (n:User{email: {email}}) ",
            "parameters": { "props" : {
                "email": "user1@learningcypher.com"
            }
        }
        } ]
    }
    ```

    2. The server will return the JSON code answer with a property named commit that contains the endpoint to invoke to commit the transaction. The result will be as follows:

    ```
    {
        "commit" : "http://localhost:7474/db/data/transaction/32/
          commit",
        "results" : [ {
            ...
    ```

    3. By sending a statement payload, like the previous one, to the http://localhost:7474/db/data/transaction/32 endpoint, you'll perform queries in that transaction.

    4. By sending a statement to the commit endpoint, you'll get the server to commit all changes made in that transaction.

- The second one is by using batch operations. Batch operations allow you to merge multiple REST API calls in only one call, which is executed atomically. You have to invoke the db/data/batch endpoint with a payload built with multiple REST API calls serialized in the JSON code. Every call must have an ID. This is described in the following code snippet:

    ```
    [ {
        "method" : "PUT",
        "to" : "/cypher",
        "body" : {
            "query" : "CREATE (n:User{email: {email}}) "
        },
        "id" : 0
    },
    ...
    ```

# Avoiding unnecessary clauses

Both DISTINCT and ORDER BY clauses can be very slow on large datasets because they scan the whole dataset and execute comparisons to sort or to distinguish unique values. You should avoid using them when it is not necessary. The ORDER BY clause in Cypher is optimized for performance so that only the final dataset (which is typically a lot smaller) is handled by the Cypher engine and ordered. The DISTINCT clause, on the other hand, can also be used in the middle of a query; so, it can act on large datasets. To clarify, let's see an example.

Suppose that the users of our social network can join groups, namely communities for users interested in certain topics. A group is a node with the Group label and has a name string property. This is shown in the following screenshot:

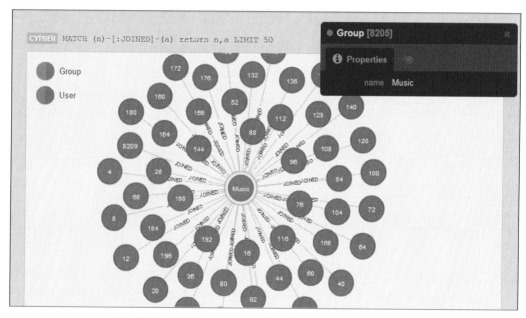

Graph visualization: some users (50) that joined the Music group

Now consider the following query:

```
MATCH (user:User) -[:JOINED]- (group:Group)
WITH DISTINCT user, group
RETURN group.name, COUNT(user)
```

This is a report about the size of each group according to the number of users who joined the group. It first looks for users related to any group, then takes the distinct user-group pairs, and finally counts the users per group name. For several reasons, this query can easily become very slow in a huge dataset. It is not scalable. Note the DISTINCT keyword in the middle of the code; maybe the person who wrote this query thought that it was necessary to consider only one user-group pair and not duplicated relationships. However, if in our application, a user can join a group only once, then the DISTINCT keyword is useless and is much expensive in terms of performance. This is because it forces the engine to run through the entire dataset and takes only distinct values. Therefore, it's important that you structure your queries so that the engine works with as little data as possible.

# Specifying the direction of relationships and variable length paths

Another important point when making the graph is to ensure that data does not require expansive query operations, and then take advantage of the structure to avoid those expansive query operations. In fact, let's continue working on the same dataset and consider the following query:

```
MATCH (user:User) -[:JOINED*]- (group:Group)
WITH user, COUNT(group) as countG
RETURN avg(countG)
```

This is a report of the average number of groups joined per user. The query considers all users connected to any group through a variable length path of the JOINED type, then counts the number of groups per user, and finally returns the average of this number.

There are two improvements that can be done to this query to improve the performance, and they both are in the first row. The first issue is that the direction of the JOINED relationship is not specified. This means that the Cypher engine must traverse the graph to search both users that joined any group and groups that joined any user. However, clearly the latter does not make any sense and, in fact, the Cypher engine won't find any such groups. This is because in our application, users can join groups but never vice versa. So, we can improve the query by specifying the direction of the relationship, for example, MATCH (user:User) -[:JOINED*]-> (group:Group).

The second issue is the variable length path (*) in the relationship pattern. The variable length path mentioned here is useless in our application if the JOINED relationship can involve only users and groups, and its direction can be only from a user to a group. In fact, if you look at the preceding screenshot, you will see that every path between a user and a group with a relationship of the JOINED type will only have length of one. Therefore, we can safely remove the variable length path. This is described in the following query:

```
MATCH (user:User) -[:JOINED]-> (group:Group)
WITH user, COUNT(group) as countG
RETURN avg(countG)
```

This is a huge improvement because the variable length path searches can be really slow operations in huge datasets. This is because the Cypher engine must match the path with a complex pattern. By running each query 2000 times and comparing the time elapsed, you'll get a result as shown in the following output code (of course, the exact time duration depends on the speed and the state of your machine):

```
Group count average - naive
duration: 90109.287146 ms
Group count average - optimized
duration: 63804.844214 ms
```

The latter query is almost 30 percent faster. This doesn't mean that you shouldn't use variable length relationship patterns at all. However, while working with huge datasets, you must use them with caution to avoid performance issues.

Generally speaking, when you face a performance issue, what you can do is use your knowledge about the domain of your application and reduce the work for Cypher. This is one reason why profiling your queries is so important, and it is the topic of the next section.

# Profiling queries

When we have users who complain of poor performance, the first step is profiling our application. Nowadays, every programming language can be profiled to look for the cause of poor performance. It's an important step because it lets us focus only on the correct cause of the performance decay that the users are experiencing. The risk, in fact, is to go on a wild goose chase, trying to optimize functions and queries that don't affect the whole performance of the application in a relevant way. Above all, we do not have an objective measure of the improvements that we get.

Therefore, suppose that we use a profiler, that is specific to our programming language (either Java, PHP, Ruby, or anything else), and we found that the code executing the following query is very slow:

```
MATCH(n:User {email:'user300@learningcypher.com'})
RETURN n
```

We need a way to profile this query to understand the operation made by the Cypher engine and its performance cost so that we can act to reduce the whole cost.

# Profiling using the Java API

If we were working with Neo4j Embedded, we would have a code that looks like the following:

```
import org.neo4j.cypher.javacompat.ExecutionEngine;
import org.neo4j.cypher.javacompat.ExecutionResult;
// ... more code
String query = "MATCH(n:User {email: {emailQuery}}) RETURN n";
Map<String,Object> params = new HashMap<>();
params.put("emailQuery", "user300@learningcypher.com");
ExecutionResult result = engine.execute(query, params);
```

Neo4j provides a way to evaluate the performance of a query. The `ExecutionEngine` class has the `profile` method, which returns an `ExecutionResult` object with profiling statistics. Invoke it in the same way you call the `execute` object. This is described in the following code snippet:

```
ExecutionResult result = engine.profile(query, params);
```

The only difference is that we can now invoke the `executionPlanDescription` method of the `ExecutionResult` object. This method is always present in the `ExecutionResult` class but can be invoked only once the query is profiled, not when the query is merely executed; calling this method after an `execute` call will cause an exception to be thrown. Now, consider the following query:

```
result.dumpToString();
PlanDescription planDescription =
                result.executionPlanDescription();
```

We called the `dumpToString` function before accessing the execution plan because it is available only after the result is enumerated. From *Chapter 1*, *Querying Neo4j Effectively with Pattern Matching*, you will remember that the `ExecutionResult` instance can be enumerated in three ways: via either the `dumpToString` or `columnAs` functions or an iterator function. Whichever you use is fine, you just need to enumerate the result before requesting the execution plan.

# Inside the execution plan description

The execution plan informs us about the operations made by the execution engine to perform our query. We can dump the string representation of the plan. This is described in the following code snippet:

```
System.out.println(res.executionPlanDescription().toString());
```

For the `MATCH(n:User {email: {emailQuery}}) RETURN n` query, we get the following result:

```
Filter(pred="Property(n,email(0)) == {emailQuery}", _rows=1,
_db_hits=1000)
NodeByLabel(identifier="n", _db_hits=0, _rows=1000, label="User",
identifiers=["n"], producer="NodeByLabel")
```

What can we gather from this result? We have the following two steps:

- `NodeByLabel`: This step means that the Cypher engine selected all nodes using a label; the label of course is `User` and the identifier to match is n. This operation processed 1000 rows (all the users we have in our database). A very important information is the number of database hits. This represents the number of the potential disk accesses to perform this step; the greater the number, the worse is the performance of the query.

- `Filter`: This step represents the filtering operation on the set that was returned by the previous operation. This has 1000 database hits.

So, the problem in this query resides in the way we are filtering our dataset.

# Profiling with Neo4j Shell

**Neo4j Shell** is a great tool to monitor and interact with a running Neo4j Server. It can be used for profiling by performing the following steps:

1. In Windows, to start the shell, you have to launch the `Neo4jShell.bat` file in the `bin` folder of the `Installation` folder, while in Linux, you have to launch the `neo4-shell` bash script.

    Neo4j Shell is not provided with the Windows installer of the Neo4j Community. To get it, you have to download the `.zip` binary from `http://www.neo4j.org/download/other_versions`.

2. Once it is started and ready, Neo4j Shell shows a command prompt. It supports many commands. You can get a list of them by typing `help`.

3. Using the `profile` command, you can instruct Neo4j Shell to perform a Cypher query, dump the result to the screen, and show the execution plan of the query. The syntax is simple: `profile <query>;`. For example, typing in the following command will give the result shown in the following screenshot. Note that you have to put the semicolon after the Cypher query to mark the end of the command:

```
profile MATCH(n{email:"user30@learningcypher.com"}) RETURN
n;
```

```
neo4j-sh (?)$ PROFILE MATCH(n {email:"user3@learningcypher.com"}) RETURN n;
+-----------------------------------------------------------------+
| n                                                               |
+-----------------------------------------------------------------+
| Node[8212]{email:"user3@learningcypher.com",userId:3}           |
+-----------------------------------------------------------------+
1 row

Filter(pred="Property(n.email(0)) == Literal(user3@learningcypher.com)", _rows=1
, _db_hits=1004)
AllNodes(identifier="n", _db_hits=1004, _rows=1004, identifiers=["n"], producer=
"AllNodes")
neo4j-sh (?)$
```

# Profiling with the REST API

To obtain the execution plan and statistics, the POST request that is made to the server must be changed. We need to enable the `profile` option by setting it to `true` in the request. Our new POST request is `/db/data/cypher?profile=true`.

You can try it in any REST client or in Neo4j Browser. In the prompt, type in the following code:

```
:POST /db/data/cypher?profile=true {
  "query": "MATCH(n:User {email: {emailQuery}}) RETURN n.userId",
  "params": {
      "emailQuery": "user300@learningcypher.com"
    }
}
```

The only difference between the preceding query and the query in the *Profiling using the Java API* section is that in the preceding query, only the `userId` property is returned. The intention is to reduce the length of the output and reduce the bandwidth occupied by the response. The following JSON code is the result:

```
{
  "columns": ["n.userId"],
  "data": [[300]],
  "plan": {
    "name": "ColumnFilter",
    "args": {
```

```
        "symKeys": ["n", "n.userId"],
        "returnItemNames": ["n.userId"],
        "_rows": 1,
        "_db_hits": 0
      },
      "rows": 1,
      "dbHits": 0,
      "children": [{
        "name": "Extract",
        "args": {
          "symKeys": ["n"],
          "exprKeys": ["n.userId"],
          "_rows": 1,
          "_db_hits": 1
        },
        "rows": 1,
        "dbHits": 1,
        "children": [{
          "name": "Filter",
          "args": {
            "pred": "Property(n,email(0)) == {emailQuery}",
            "_rows": 1,
            "_db_hits": 1000
          },
          "rows": 1,
          "dbHits": 1000,
          "children": [{
            "name": "NodeByLabel",
            "args": {
              "identifier": "n",
              "_db_hits": 0,
              "_rows": 1000,
              "label": "User",
              "identifiers": ["n"],
              "producer": "NodeByLabel"
            },
            "rows": 1000,
            "dbHits": 0,
            "children": []
          }]
        }]
      }]
    }
  }
```

The first property (`columns`) contains the column names of the data returned as result. The second property (`data`) contains the result of the query, while the third property (`plan`) stores the execution plan.

You may have noticed that here we have the same steps as in the Java API and two more steps: `Extract` and `ColumnFilter`. They are related to the fact that we are returning only one property, not the whole node. Anyway, they are not important now because they generate a minimal number of database hits. The following screenshot shows how we can invoke the REST API:

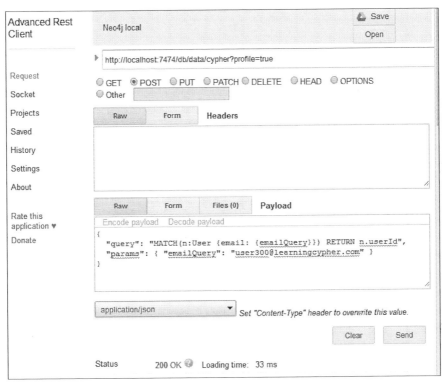

Invoking the REST API with Advanced REST client, a Chrome plugin

# Indexes and constraints

Clearly, getting all nodes and filtering them is not the best way to find a node. Every worthy database, just like Neo4j, allows you to create indexes in order to find data quickly.

From Version 2.0, in Neo4j, there is a new and recommended type of index, that is, a label index. These are the only indexes supported by Cypher. Therefore, let's create an index for users based on the `email` property. We only need to execute the following query:

```
CREATE INDEX ON :User(email)
```

As this operation of creating an index is asynchronous, we must wait for the indexes to be built and go online. A timeout of one minute for 1000 items should be enough on any modern machine. This is described in the following query:

```
try (Transaction tx = graphDb.beginTx()) {
    Schema schema = graphDb.schema();
    schema.awaitIndexesOnline(1, TimeUnit.MINUTES);
}
```

> Waiting for an index to go online can be done only with either the Java API or Neo4j Shell at the moment. This means that if you are using the REST API, you have to wait a reasonable interval of time while the server builds the index. Clearly, if you create the index before inserting any data, the index creation will be immediate and data will be indexed automatically.

Once the index is online, we can run the profiler again and dump the plan. This time, we get only one row, as shown in the following output code:

```
SchemaIndex(identifier="n", _db_hits=0, _rows=1, label="User",
query="{emailQuery}", identifiers=["n"], property="email",
producer="SchemaIndex")
```

Now, we have only one operation: `SchemaIndex`. It has no database hits and only one row is processed instead of 1000 database hits. This is a big improvement!

> Deleting an index from the database can be done with the DROP INDEX command. The syntax is similar to the CREATE INDEX command, as illustrated in the following query:
>
> ```
> DROP INDEX ON :User(email)
> ```

# SCAN hints

Now, let's see another example that allows us to introduce a new keyword. Suppose that we have a certain number of inactive users in our social network; let's say 10. We express inactive users with the `Inactive` label. The query to get all the inactive users could be the following:

```
MATCH (n:User:Inactive)
RETURN n
```

The execution plan of this query is shown in the following code:

```
Filter(pred="hasLabel(n:Inactive(2))", _rows=10, _db_hits=0)
NodeByLabel(identifier="n", _db_hits=0, _rows=1000, label="User",
identifiers=["n"], producer="NodeByLabel")
```

This means that the query is executed in two steps. They are as follows:

- In the first step, NodeByLabel, all nodes labeled User are read, which in this case is 1000 rows
- The inactive users are then filtered from the set of nodes

Note that if we invert the labels, we would read only 10 rows. The USING SCAN keyword allows you to specify the label to be scanned first. This is described in the following query:

```
MATCH (n:User:Inactive)
USING SCAN u:Inactive
RETURN n
```

The execution plan now becomes the following:

```
Filter(pred="(hasLabel(n:User(1)) AND hasLabel(n:Inactive(2)))",
_rows=10, _db_hits=0)
NodeByLabel(identifier="n", _db_hits=0, _rows=10,
label="Inactive", identifiers=["n"], producer="NodeByLabel")
```

As expected, now we are reading only 10 rows instead of 1000 rows.

# Index hints

When you write a query, Cypher will use indexes, if possible, in order to maximize the performance of the query. Therefore, usually you won't need to specify whether or not and to use an index and which one to use. Anyway, you can specify the indexes to be used to make sure that the index is used in the query. Look at the following example query:

```
MATCH(n:User)
USING INDEX n:User(email)
WHERE n.email = {emailQuery}
RETURN n.userId
```

This query makes sure that the index on the `email` property is used for searching. If the index is not present or cannot be used in the query as is, an error will be returned. Note that the `USING INDEX` clause must be specified before the `WHERE` clause that is used to filter users.

To sum up, you can put the `USING INDEX` instruction in the query when you want a certain index to be used.

# Constraints

Another interesting feature of Neo4j from Version 2.0 is the ability to create a uniqueness constraint on a specific property in a certain label. Consider the following query:

```
CREATE CONSTRAINT ON (user:User)
ASSERT user.userId IS UNIQUE
```

The preceding code ensures that there won't be two co-existing nodes that have the label `User` and the same user ID. If you try to create a `User` node with the same user ID of an existing node in the database, the database will generate an error, as shown in the following screenshot:

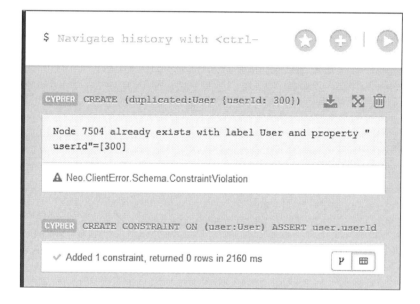

Of course, this feature is useful to guarantee the integrity of your data if your application identifies users by their user ID. You might wonder why we are talking about constraints in this chapter. The reason is because when you create a constraint, Neo4j automatically creates an index on the constrained property. In fact, try to create the index after you create the constraint with the following query:

```
CREATE INDEX ON :User(userId)
```

Now, you will get an error that informs you that the index already exists. The following result is shown:

```
Already constrained CONSTRAINT ON ( user:User ) ASSERT user.userId
IS UNIQUE.
```

Clearly, you can delete the old index and create a new constraint instead.

All in all, if you have a property that must be unique in a labeled set of nodes, create a uniqueness constraint. Besides having your data integrity guaranteed by the database, you will gain a significant performance advantage due to the index that is created along with the constraint.

# Summary

In this chapter, the focus was on Cypher performance. In the first section, we learned some best practices and several tips to avoid common performance pitfalls. Then, we learned how to read the execution plan of a Cypher query. Finally, we introduced a new feature of Neo4j 2.0: the schema. Although it is still work in progress, it can be very useful in our applications, both to preserve the integrity of our data and to assure good levels of performance.

At this point, you should know how to analyze an expensive query and how to profile it to recognize the reason of the performance decay. You should be able to change the query in order to improve its performance.

In the next chapter, we will learn, through a real-world application, how to migrate a relational database and its related SQL queries to Neo4j and Cypher.

# 5
# Migrating from SQL

For several reasons, relational databases are probably the most used storage solutions by programmers and architects. There are a lot of stable tools for designing, monitoring, and querying. Both the relational model and the SQL language that are well-known among the programmers and are a part of most programming languages, such as Java, Ruby, Scala, C# and so on, have stable drivers that allow you to connect to common SQL databases. In the past, migrating from SQL could be a nightmare; your tools would stop working, and your application (or the persistence layer at least) would need to be completely rewritten. The whole reporting system could stop working as well. Nowadays, thanks to Cypher and to projects such as **neo4j-jdbc**, (`http://www.neo4j.org/develop/tools/jdbc`), the process is much simpler.

Migrating from a commercial SQL database such as SQL Server or Oracle to a graph database could happen due to several reasons:

- The database can't scale up any more (at least with reasonable costs), because it is bombed with write requests, and your RDBMS is blocked by transactions, locks, triggers, and indexes

- Your model changes quickly in the life cycle of the application, and you can't fit your logical model in the relational model without refactoring the database schema at every change request you submit

- You spend a lot of time deploying and updating the database schema, and you're looking for more flexibility but with the guarantee provided by **ACID** transactions

Irrespective of the reasons to migrate from SQL to Cypher, in this chapter, we will learn through real-world examples how to migrate a database from a SQL database to Neo4j in three steps, which are as follows:

- Migrating the schema from SQL to Neo4j
- Migrating the data from tables to Neo4j
- Migrating queries to let your application continue working, without making too many changes to your code

In this chapter, for the sake of generality, it is assumed that the interaction with the SQL database is made directly without any ORM or an abstracting layer. In Java, this means JDBC.

Anyway, it is noteworthy that for JPA, there is a driver-enabling Neo4j for Java EE (`http://github.com/alexsmirnov/neo4j-connector`), while for Ruby, the project `Neo4j.rb` (`https://github.com/andreasronge/neo4j`) acts as compliant ActiveModel wrapper for Neo4j.

If you are using an ORM supported by Neo4j, you won't need to migrate CRUD operations, but you will still need to migrate the schema, data, and complex queries. In fact, ORMs and Active Records just reduce the frequency with which you use the underlying query languages and, foremost, save you the effort of mapping the database every time from the data model to the object model; however, you must still know your data model.

# Our example

In this chapter, as an example, we will migrate a minimal bibliography store. A bibliographic store contains a huge set of publications that can be referenced.

Our example is composed of the following entities:

- **Reference**: This can be a book, journal or conference article
- **Publisher**: This can be a company, university, organization, or conference from where the article is published.
- **Author**: This represents the author of a publication

The following figure shows the E-R diagram of the database:

An in-depth explanation of the E-R diagram would be far beyond the purpose of this book; here we can just say that the purpose of the E-R diagram is to describe a model based on entities and relationships. It shows the following features:

- **Entities**: These are the objects that have an independent existence and can be identified uniquely. They are represented in a box.
- **Attributes**: These are the values whose existence depends on an entity; an attribute does not make sense alone and must be related to an entity. They are represented in a circle linked to an entity. An attribute has a multiple cardinality if it can have multiple values. In this case, the attribute is represented in a double circle, like the Tags attribute in the previous diagram..
- **Relations**: This is the relation between entities. They are represented in a diamond.

This application is similar to a book store. The difference is that it can contain much more data such as articles, websites, blog posts and so on. However, the most important difference is that you can have huge number of relationships:

- A reference can be published by a publisher
- An author may have worked on many references
- A reference can be cited in many other references

It's important to understand the domain we are migrating because we will change the persistence model extensively; however, the domain model will remain the invariant part and will continue to be the basis of the new data layer. In the next step, we will migrate the schema of this database to Neo4j.

# Migrating the schema

The database schema in a relational database defines tables, attributes (columns), primary and foreign keys, as well as indexes. To create these schema elements in relational databases, you will need a **Data Description Language (DDL)**.

In the code provided at the Packt Publishing website (http://www.packtpub.com/), you will find the complete code to create and query the database.

The queries shown in this chapter are slightly different from the ones provided with the code. In fact, the complete code uses the **Apache Derby** (a famous embedded SQL database) and, just as most relational databases, has its own dialect. For generality, the SQL code shown in the chapter, is SQL ANSI, which is the standard SQL.

Moreover, the SQL queries in this chapter are written in lowercase to better differentiate them from the Cypher queries. As you know, both SQL and Cypher are case insensitive.

For example, the following CREATE TABLE SQL query creates a table of the reference entries in the database:

```
create table ReferenceEntries(
    ID int not null primary key,
    TITLE varchar(200) not null,
    ABSTRACTTEXT varchar(1000) not null,
    PUBLISHEDBY varchar(200)
        references PUBLISHERS(NAME)
            on delete set null
            on update restrict,
    PublishedYear int)
```

The table has a primary key (ID), a non-nullable property (title), and the column that contains the abstract. This table also references the publisher and the data of this relation (the year). This relation is present here and not in a new table because it's a one-to-one relation.

As you know, representing an E-R diagram in SQL is not straightforward. For example, to represent the reference entity, we need another table, one that stores the tags of a reference entry because SQL does not allow multivalue attributes:

```
create table EntryTags(
      ReferenceId int references ReferenceEntries(ID),
      Tag VARCHAR(50)  )
```

Note that this table does not need a primary key (though it could have one) because it does not store entities.

The following diagram shows all tables used in our application to represent the aforementioned E-R diagram:

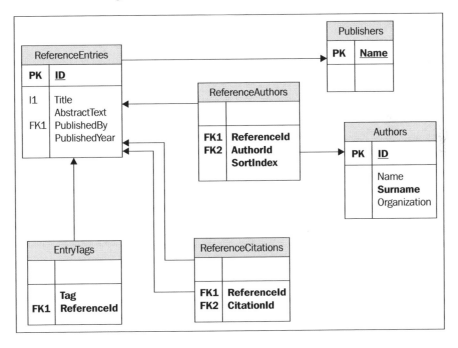

What do we need to migrate this schema? Even though Neo4j essentially is considered schema-less, it is still better to consider designing the graph model in advance by making the following important choices:

- Determining the type of labels and the number of labels to use in our graph database
- Determining the properties that need unique assertions
- Determining the properties that need indexing
- Determining the relationships to consider between the nodes

I think that the best approach is to start from the E-R diagram of the database. If you do not have an E-R diagram for your database, you could easily write one; however, for this, you should know the domain of the application. In the next sections, we will answer the questions that just arose.

# Labels

Since entities are objects that are not defined by their attributes but have an identity of their own, you must be able to identify them in the graph. For each entity in the E-R diagram, create a label.

Therefore, in our example database to migrate, we have the following labels:

- Author
- Reference
- Publisher

Note that the entities in a E-R model don't match one-to-one with tables because many relations (and surely many-to-many relations) are mapped in tables. So, it's better to create the Neo4j model from a more real model (like the E-R model) rather than from the table-based model, This prevents the risk of introducing complexity and limitations of RDBMS in the Neo4j graph.

Just like when you translate from an E-R model into SQL, you can merge two entities that have a one-to-one relationship in a single label. Of course, this choice depends on the domain of your application and the usage of your database.

To clarify, consider a diagram with two entities, Person and Personal Account, each with their attributes and sharing a one-to-one relationship between them. This means that creating or deleting a person will always result in creating or deleting a bank account and vice versa:

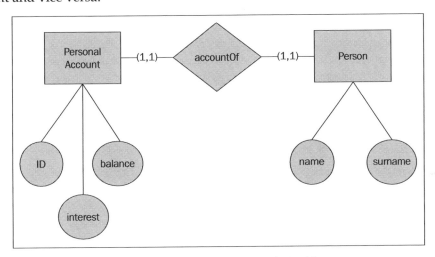

The E-R diagram of a one-to-one relationship

In this case, you could decide to put everything inside the **Person** label:

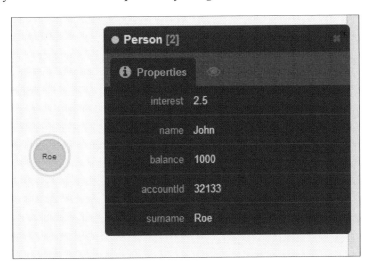

On the other hand, you could put two labels in the database (Person and Personal bank account) and a relationship between them. In this case, you can decide later whether most of **Person** nodes will also have the **PersonalAccount** label because even Neo4j allows self-loops:

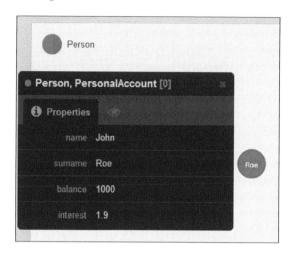

Of course this approach, though being very flexible, would affect all your queries and their performance because you will always need to visit a relationship to get the account information of a person. In fact, you can't say that the data in these labels are in the same node of a priori. The best approach depends on the usage of the database—if your application reads the **PersonalAccount** data every time it accesses the **Person** data, then they should be merged.

# Indexes and constraints

Now, let's go to the second and third question about indexes and constraints. We can ignore attributes now because Neo4j is schema-less. But, we can define the uniqueness constraints. In the previous chapter, we had seen how these constraints are useful to preserve database integrity, and improve performances of queries. For example, for the reference label:

```
CREATE CONSTRAINT ON (r:Reference)
ASSERT r.id IS UNIQUE
```

The same constraint can be created for authors:

```
CREATE CONSTRAINT ON (r:Author)
ASSERT r.id IS UNIQUE
```

Considering, our model publishers don't have an ID but are referenced by name, we can create a constraint on the name:

```
CREATE CONSTRAINT ON (r:Publisher)
ASSERT r.name IS UNIQUE
```

Then, we can create an index on the properties most used for searching. We mustn't create indexes for properties that have a constraint already defined, because a constraint implies an index automatically as we learnt in the previous chapter. But, for example, the title property will be surely used for searching:

```
CREATE INDEX ON :Reference(title)
```

Also, tags are likely to be used for searching:

```
CREATE INDEX ON :Reference(tags)
```

While, authors could be searched by surname:

```
CREATE INDEX ON :Author(surname)
```

Publishers nowadays don't need any index, because the name is already indexed by the constraint we defined in the preceding code.

> Note that by using SQL databases, you have to create one more table to express multi-valued attributes such as the tags of the reference. By using Neo4j, this is not necessary because you can have array properties on nodes and relationships. Anyway, you can still create a separate tag node for each tag and link it to the reference through a relation if you should find that such a model performs better in your situation. Yet, this choice would neither be driven by data model nor by database limitations, but only by performance or applicative considerations.

To summarize, the answer to the second and third questions are:

- Create a uniqueness constraint on properties that are the primary keys of the SQL model
- Create an index on properties that are used for searching, and probably have an index on the SQL database

# Relationships

The last question is which relationships to use. Since relationships in Neo4j are complex structures with properties and types, you don't have to create anything like relation tables as we did in SQL to describe many-to-many relations or relations with attributes. The consequence is that relationships between entities of the E-R model can be expressed directly as Neo4j relationships in the graph.

In our application, we have these relationships:

- AuthoredBy
- Cites
- PublishedBy

In my opinion, the resulting Neo4j database has a far more natural look than its SQL ancestor, especially if we compare them to the E-R diagram. The reason is that this domain fits the graph model more naturally than the table model. In this case, querying and data manipulation also looks easier, it will be clearer in the next sections of this chapter. The old motto "use the right tool for the job" is still valid. In fact, SQL is still a very good choice for data that doesn't have too many multiple entity relations.

# Migrating the data

To migrate the data, you have to convert SQL data to graph data. This is a long-lasting activity of the process and probably awkward as well. Because you have to migrate data from SQL, you must read data using ad hoc SQL queries and write data using Cypher queries.

Note that another strategy would be importing data from a CSV file, with the LOAD CSV FROM statement, which is available from Cypher 2.1 at `http://docs.neo4j.org/chunked/milestone/import-importing-data-from-a-single-csv-file.html`.

# Entities

Because we have to create a node with its attributes, we have to read data using a SQL statement that returns all the data we need to create a node. Of course, you can migrate an entity in more steps, but we would usually prefer to perform only one CREATE query for performance reasons because otherwise we would have to migrate a huge database.

1. For example, let's start by migrating the `Authors` entity. This entity is easy to deal with; in fact, all attributes are only in one table:

```
select ID, NAME, SURNAME
  from AUTHORS
```

This SQL query returns all the `Authors` entities in the database. Now, we have to iterate on each returned row to create a new node per row:

```
CREATE (:Author { id: {id},
                  name: {name},
                  surname: {surname} })
```

Clearly, this is the perfect situation to use parameters. In fact, we will run a lot of similar queries and take advantage of the cached execution plans as this will give a boost to the migration, as we learned in the previous chapter.

2. We can deal with the `Publisher` entity in the same way. Let's start reading from the table:

```
select NAME
  from Publishers
```

Then, we can create a node for each returned row using the same parameters:

```
CREATE (:Publisher { name: {name} })
```

3. Assuming that we have chosen to store tags in an array property, the first problem is when we have to create the `Reference` entities. In the SQL database, in fact, the entity is split into two tables, so the migration must be done in two steps: creating the Reference nodes and then setting the tag property on the node.

For the first step, we need to load the references from the database:

```
select ID, TITLE, ABSTRACTTEXT
  from REFERENCEENTRIES
```

Then we need to create the nodes:

```
CREATE (:Reference { id: {id},
                     title: {title},
                     abstractText: {abstractText} })
```

For the second step, we need to query the SQL database again. For each reference found in the first step, we must query the database to get the tags of that reference:

```
select TAG
  from EntryTags
 where ReferenceId = ?
```

The ID of the reference is passed as the SQL parameter. Once we have got the tags of a reference, we have to update the node, setting the `tags` property, which is shown in the following code:

```
MATCH (r:Reference{id: {id}})
  SET r.tags = {tags}
```

Of course, you could also build a single command to create the node and set its tags at one time instead of performing two Cypher queries:

```
CREATE (:Reference{ id: {id},
                    title: {title},
                    abstractText: {abstractText},
                    tags: {tags} })
```

# Relationships

Well, now we have migrated all the entities, it's time to migrate relationships. The following are the steps:

1. The easiest relation to migrate is the one between cited references. We must look into the `ReferenceCitations` table:

```
select CitationId
  from ReferenceCitations
 where ReferenceId = ?
```

By iterating the result set, we have to create a relationship for every row:

```
MATCH (r:Reference{id: {idRef}}),
      (c:Reference{id: {idCit}})
CREATE (r)-[:Cites]->(c)
```

This query will find the involved nodes and will create the relationship between them.

2. Migrating the relation between the `Reference` entity and the `Publisher` entity is easy as well. We can read for each reference the publisher information as follows:

```
select ID, PublishedYear, PublishedBy
from ReferenceEntries
```

Then, we can store this information as a relationship in the right node:

```
MATCH (r:Reference{id: {id}})
MERGE (p:Publisher{name: {pubId}})
CREATE (r)-[:PublishedBy {year: {publishedYear}}]->(p)
```

The preceding query only works if a Reference node is found with the given ID. If so, it finds the publisher with the given name or creates a name, if the Reference node is not found. Finally, it creates a relationship between them. An important thing you can note is that unlike SQL databases, Neo4j cannot do anything to guarantee that you will have only one publisher per reference. This is a responsibility that now rests at the application level. What you can do is delete all publishers related to a reference before creating any relationship with the following code:

```
MATCH (:Reference{id: {id}}) -[r:PublishedBy]->()
DELETE r
```

You can put this query and the previous one in a transaction to ensure that you do not leave the database in a strange state (a reference without any publisher). This can also be achieved in a single query:

```
MATCH (a:Reference { id: {id} })
OPTIONAL MATCH (a)-[r:PublishedBy]->()
WITH a, r
MERGE (p:Publisher { name: {pubId} })
CREATE (a)-[:PublishedBy { year: {publishedYear} }]->(p)
DELETE r
```

The preceding query will find the reference with the given ID and, optionally, the existing `PublishedBy` relation. Then, it will create the new relation and finally it will delete the old relation, if it exists.

3. The approach to migrate the relation between the `Reference` and `Authors` entity is similar. First of all, we must read `Authors` for each `Reference` entity:

```
select ID, NAME, SURNAME
  from AUTHORS
  join ReferenceAuthors
    on ReferenceAuthors.AuthorId = Authors.Id
 where ReferenceId = ?
 order by SortOrder
```

Now, we can create the relationships:

```
MATCH (r:Reference{id: {id}})
MERGE (a:Author {id: {authorId},
                 name: {name},
                 surname: {surname} })
CREATE (r)-[:AuthoredBy{sortIndex: {sortIndex}}]->(a)
```

This query is similar to the query used to link a publisher to a reference; it creates the `Authors` entity if it is not present in the database. Note that the `sortIndex` value is set in the relationship, and it is deduced since we ordered the SQL query by the `SortOrder` value.

# Migrating queries

Since Neo4j supports ACID transactions, you won't need to change the infrastructure of your application to simulate a transaction (this will be required if we are migrating from SQL to a non-transactional database), but you will still need to rewrite your queries.

# CRUD

First and foremost, we must migrate the **Create**, **Read**, **Update**, and **Delete** ( **CRUD** ) queries. We already did this step in the previous section, but we overlooked a point—how do we migrate auto-incremented IDs (identities) from SQL to Neo4j? You could use the node ID generated and autoincremented by Neo4j. Yet, as we noticed in *Chapter 1, Querying Neo4j Effectively with Pattern Matching*, Neo4j could recompute the node IDs, and you should not trust them. If you really need an auto-incremented reliable ID, you will have to simulate the creation of an auto-incremented ID. Suppose we want to create an `Author` entity, and we want the application to set the next available ID. For this, we can write the following code:

```
CREATE (a:Author { name: {name},
                   surname: {surname} })
SET a.id = ID(a)
RETURN a.id
```

The preceding query is formed in two steps: in the first step, it creates the `Author` entity with the name and surname, then in the second, it sets the `id` property to the Neo4j internal ID. The internal ID is so fixed once for all in the `id` property, and you can use it externally from Neo4j in your application code.

Note that the uniqueness of the `id` property is also guaranteed by the constraint we already created in the previous section.

To summarize from the previous section, you will gather that:

- SQL `insert` queries become `CREATE` or `MATCH ... SET` queries in Cypher while working with multivalue attributes
- SQL `update` queries become `MATCH ... SET` queries in Cypher

We miss the `delete` SQL clause. For example, let's delete one `Author` entity from the database:

```
delete from Authors
where ID = ?
```

Of course, this will generate a constraint violation error if the `Author` entity is linked to a reference, and the relation is assured by a foreign key constraint, as usually is the case. The effect is the same if we delete the `Author` entity with Cypher, and the `Author` entity is related to a `Reference` node:

```
MATCH (a:Author { id: {id}})
DELETE a
```

In fact, in Neo4j, all nodes have an implicit constraint—a node can't be deleted if it is related to any other node.

You have to perform two queries in SQL to delete the `Author` entity with its relationships, while with Cypher, one query with `OPTIONAL MATCH` is enough:

```
MATCH (a:Author { id: {id}})
OPTIONAL MATCH (a)-[r]-()
DELETE a, r
```

We already saw this type of query in *Chapter 3, Manipulating the Database*.

# Searching queries

To be suitable for a useful application, besides CRUD operations, the database should support the following queries:

- The list of references found by titles
- The list of all reference entries with a given tag

Consider the first item, that is, the query to find a reference entry, when its title is given. In SQL, this will be:

```
select * from REFERENCEENTRIES
where title like '%Neo4j%'
```

It looks for references that have a title with the word Neo4j in it.

The LIKE clause of SQL can be easily translated in Cypher using regular expressions:

```
MATCH (a:Reference)
WHERE a.title =~ '.*Neo4j.*'
RETURN a
```

If the SQL database is not case sensitive (for example, SQL server), the WHERE clause must be changed to WHERE a.title =~ '(?i).*Neo4j.*'. For more details about regular expressions supported by Cypher, please refer to *Chapter 2, Filter, Aggregate, and Combine Results*.

 A regular expressions search is still not supported by indexes. Although this limitation will be removed in a next release, at the moment, every time you perform a text search based on a regular expression, Cypher will run through the whole dataset to collect items that fulfill the filter even though the property is indexed.

Now, let's take a look at the following example that has the list of references with a certain tag. In SQL, the query would need to make a join and look into the EntryTags tables:

```
select ReferenceEntries.*
  from EntryTags
  join ReferenceEntries
    on ReferenceEntries.ID = EntryTags.ReferenceId
  where Tag = 'Neo4j'
```

The query is shorter and more readable in Cypher:

```
MATCH (r:Reference)
WHERE ANY ( tag IN r.tags WHERE tag = 'Neo4j' )
RETURN r
```

This query will search the tag Neo4j in the array property tags of references. The Cypher query is simpler because in SQL, we had to introduce a table to store a multivalue attribute and this is not needed in Neo4j.

# Grouping queries

A minimal set of analysis queries needed for our application is as follows:

- The list of most-cited references that have a certain tag
- The list of most-cited authors, each with a number of citations

The first query is complex in SQL. It is given as follows:

```
select Id, CNT
 from (
select ReferenceEntries.Id,
       Count(ReferenceCitations.ReferenceId) as CNT
  from EntryTags
  join ReferenceEntries
    on ReferenceEntries.ID = EntryTags.ReferenceId
  join ReferenceCitations
    on ReferenceCitations.CitationId = ReferenceEntries.Id
  where Tag = 'Neo4j'
  group by ReferenceEntries.Id
 ) refQ
 order by refQ.CNT desc
```

The preceding SQL query needs to be split into two parts. It needs an inner part to select the references and count the number of citations it has in other references. Note that this part needs two joins: to `tags` and to `citations`. Then, the outer query will sort the references in a descending order to show the most cited at the top of the list. This split is required only because an `orderby`-clause together with the `groupby`-clause is not supported by all RDBMS.

The simpler the model, the simpler the queries. In fact, the same query in Cypher is far shorter and easier to read. It is given as follows:

```
MATCH (r:Reference) <-[cit:Cites]- (:Reference)
WHERE ANY ( tag IN r.tags WHERE tag = 'Neo4j' )
RETURN r, COUNT(cit) as cnt
ORDER BY cnt DESC
```

This query matches the `Reference-Citations` relationship, filtering nodes by tag, and returns the starting nodes and the count of their citations in other documents. Finally, the dataset is sorted by this number.

The last query to migrate is the list of the most-cited authors entity, each with its number of cited articles. This is the SQL query, where the differences with the previous one are highlighted:

```
select AuthorId, CNT
 from (
select ReferenceAuthors.AuthorId,
       Count(ReferenceCitations.ReferenceId) as CNT
  from EntryTags
  join ReferenceEntries
```

```
      on ReferenceEntries.ID = EntryTags.ReferenceId
   join ReferenceCitations
      on ReferenceCitations.CitationId = ReferenceEntries.Id
   join ReferenceAuthors
      on ReferenceAuthors.ReferenceId = ReferenceEntries.Id
   group by ReferenceAuthors.AuthorId
   ) refQ
    order by refQ.CNT desc
```

The most-cited authors entity has one more join to the relation table of authors, but the grouping clause is different. The Cypher query is also similar to the previous one, which is as follows:

```
MATCH (a:Author)<-[aut:AuthoredBy]-(r:Reference)<-[cit:Cites]-
(:Reference),
RETURN a, COUNT(cit) as cnt
ORDER BY cnt DESC
```

The main difference (highlighted in the code) is that we added one more MATCH expression to get the Authors entity of each reference.

From this example, we can generalize that in the SQL query for each JOIN with an entity, the Cypher query will have a MATCH expression.

# Summary

In this final chapter, we learned a practical approach to migrate a database from SQL to Neo4j.

We started migrating the database schema. We saw that the migration will be straightforward if we think more in terms of entities and relations (E-R)than in terms of tables and columns. In other words, if we come back to the relational model, the entities will become nodes, while the relations will become graph relationships. The attributes will become properties.

Then, we migrated the data. We started migrating entities with their attributes, and then we migrated the relations. During this task, we learned how to migrate CRUD queries from SQL to Cypher.

Finally, we migrated some complex queries used in a real-world application. We learned how to migrate searching queries (in place of LIKE we have regular expressions in Cypher) and grouping queries.

This was the last chapter. Now, you should be able to use Cypher with any real-world application you want to develop, from design to implementation to tuning performances.

When you need a short and quick reference to all the Cypher clauses and patterns you learned in this book, I suggest you read the Neo4j Cypher refcard at (`http://docs.neo4j.org/refcard/2.0/`). In additions to this, the *Appendix* contains a detailed list of all the operators and almost all functions supported by Cypher.

# Operators and Functions

This appendix is a brief introduction to the operators and functions supported by Cypher 2.0.1. For each operator or function, we will see a brief description, an example, and some usage notes.

The queries are performed on an example database of books that have labels and relationships described in *Chapter 2, Filter, Aggregate, and Combine Results*. Sometimes, I used the HR management tool database (from *Chapter 1, Querying Neo4j Effectively with Pattern Matching*) when it would be more appropriate.

To try out the code, you can set up the database with the scripts, which you can download from the Packt Publishing website (`http://www.packtpub.com/support`).

## Operators

The operators are grouped by category. Most of them return a `null` value if any operand has a `null` value. Anyway, there are some exceptions. So, for each operator, the behavior in case of a `null` value operand is specified.

## Comparison operators

Comparison operators are binary operators that return a Boolean or a `null` value as results. They are mostly used in the `WHERE` clause (see *Chapter 2, Filter, Aggregate, and Combine Results*, for details) to filter data according to a condition, although they can be used in the `RETURN` clause as well.

In Cypher, comparison operators can be grouped in two classes: ordering operators and equality operators.

# Ordering operators

Ordering operators are used to compare values (usually property values or literals). They are as follows:

| Operator | Description |
|----------|-------------|
| < | Less than |
| <= | Less than or equal to |
| > | Greater than |
| >= | Greater than or equal to |

Let's see an example using one of these operators. This query looks for all books published in 2012 or later. If a `PublishedBy` relationship doesn't have the `year` property set, it will be discarded. The query is as follows:

```
MATCH (a:Book)-[r:PublishedBy]-(b:Publisher)
WHERE r.year >= 2012
RETURN a,r,b
```

Note the following outcomes:

- Only numbers and string values are supported.

- Comparing any value to a `null` value will result in a `null` value. For example, all of the following expressions will give a `null` value:

  - `1 < NULL`

  - `NULL < "String"`

  - `NULL < NULL`

- Comparing nodes or relationships is an illegal operation. It will result in a syntax error.

- Comparing numbers of different types (a double value with an integer value or a long value with an integer value) is supported; however, numbers will be converted before being compared.

- Comparing arrays is not supported.

- Comparing numbers to string values will generate a runtime error. If you don't know whether a property is a number in the dataset and if a string comparison is enough, you can resort to the `STR` function (this is covered later in this appendix).

# Equality operators

Equality operators are used to test the equality of two values. They return a Boolean value or a `null` value. They are as follows:

- `=` returns `true` if the two values are equal
- `<>` returns `true` if the two values are not equal

The following query returns the books that have the specified title:

```
MATCH (a:Book)
WHERE a.title = "Learning Cypher"
RETURN a
```

Note the following:

- Comparing any value to a `null` value will result in a `null` value. To test `null` values, use the NULL equality operators mentioned in the next section. For example, all of the following expressions will give a `null` value as the result:
    - `230.0 = NULL`
    - `NULL = "String"`
    - `NULL = NULL`

- Comparing values of properties of different types is supported and will always return `false`, except for the numbers that will be converted before the comparison.

>  Because of this important difference with ordering operators, changing from an equality operator to a sorting operator and vice versa should be done carefully in order to avoid unexpected results.

- String comparison is case sensitive.
- Nodes, relationships, and paths can be compared for equality as well, as explained in the following list:
    - Two nodes are equal only if they are the same node
    - Two relationships are equal only if they are the same relationship
    - Two paths are equal only if they contain both the same nodes and the same relationships

- Comparing either a node, a relationship, or a path to a property value (number or string) will generate a syntax error.

## NULL equality operators

The operators IS NULL and IS NOT NULL are used to check whether a value is a null value. These operators always return a Boolean value. They are mostly used to check whether or not a property is set in a node or in a relationship. The following query returns all books that have a title property:

```
MATCH (b:Book)
WHERE b.title IS NOT NULL
RETURN b
```

All values can be tested; not only node properties and relationship properties but also nodes, relationships, and paths.

# Mathematical operators

Mathematical operators work with number values. They are binary operators except the unary minus (-). The binary operators are +, -, *, /, %, and ^. Consider the following query:

```
MATCH (a)-[r:PublishedBy]-(b)
WHERE r.year % 2 = 1
RETURN -2^ 1.0 * COUNT(DISTINCT a) / COUNT(DISTINCT b)
```

This query performs an example mathematical operation on the number of distinct books per publisher.

Note the following:

- Every operator will return a null value if any operand is a NULL value. Refer to the COALESCE function, described in a later section, to deal with the default values in case of a null value.

- Every operator will throw an exception if any operand is not a number, except for the + operator. This also holds true for strings and collections, but with a different meaning (see the next section).

# The concatenation operator

Both strings and collections have the + operator. It is used to concatenate items to strings and collections. Consider the following query:

```
RETURN "Hello" + " Cypher " + 2
```

This simple query just concatenates some strings. The number 2 is converted to string just before being concatenated. Now consider the following query:

```
MATCH (aa:Book)
RETURN aa.tags + ["book","found"]
```

This query, for each book in the database, returns a collection computed by concatenating the book's tags with a fixed collection of tags.

Note the following:

- This operator returns a `null` value if any operand is a `null` value.
- When concatenating strings, the + operator will try to convert the operand to string, except when an operand is a collection. In this case, the result will be in a new collection with the string concatenated.

# The IN operator

The `IN` predicate is used to check whether a given value is in a collection of items. It returns either a Boolean value or a `null` value if any operand has a `null` value. Consider the following query:

```
MATCH (aa:Book)
WHERE 'drama' IN (aa.tags)
RETURN aa.title
```

This query returns all books that have the word *drama* in their tags.

# Regular expressions

To check whether a string value matches a regular expression, use the =~ operator. This operator is explained in detail in *Chapter 2, Filter, Aggregate, and Combine Results*. As a reminder, following is an example query that looks for books that contain the word *tale*:

```
MATCH (aa:Book)
WHERE aa.title =~ "(?i).*tale.*"
RETURN aa
```

# Functions

Functions are grouped by usage. Except for the COALESCE function, all of these functions return a `null` value if any argument has a `null` value.

# COALESCE

The COALESCE function takes any number of parameters (at least one) and returns the first non-null value. It returns a null value only in case all the parameters have null values.

Usually, this function is used every time you have to deal with null values and want a fallback value in case of a null value. Consider the following query:

```
MATCH (aa:Book)
WHERE 'novel' IN COALESCE(aa.tags, ['novel'])
RETURN aa.title
```

This query returns all books that have *novel* in their tags, but will return all the books that do not have no tags set as well. In fact, if a book doesn't have the tags property, the COALESCE function will return the collection ['novel']. Therefore, the IN predicate will always succeed.

# TIMESTAMP

The TIMESTAMP function takes no arguments and returns the number of milliseconds passed from the midnight of January 1, 1970. This function is used when you create or update a node to mark the change in the date. It is especially useful to create versions. Consider the following query:

```
CREATE (a:Book {title: "Learning Cypher", version: TIMESTAMP() })
```

This query creates a book in the database setting the version number as a timestamp. Another query could check whether the version of the book has not changed before updating, and fail if a new version of the book is in the database (an optimistic lock).

# ID

The ID function returns the identification number, managed by Neo4j, of a node or a relationship. Consider the following query:

```
MATCH (a)
RETURN a
ORDER BY ID(a)
LIMIT 1
```

The preceding query returns the node with the minimum ID value. In fact, it sorts the dataset by the ID, then limits the results to one row.

# Working with nodes

The following functions are specific to nodes. They are commonly used when you work with paths or collections of nodes and you want to inspect nodes and labels.

## NODES

The NODES function returns a collection of all the nodes in a path. It is used when you want all the nodes found traversing a path between two nodes. Consider the following query:

```
MATCH p = (:Employee {surname: "Davies"})-[:REPORTS_TO*]-
          (:Employee {surname: "Taylor"})
RETURN NODES(p)
```

The preceding query first matches all the paths between two employees, visiting all the relations of the REPORTS_TO type and then returns all the nodes visited. In other words, it returns all the employees found in a hierarchy between two employees.

Note that, being a collection, the return value can be further inspected with the collection functions, which is explained later.

## LABELS

To get all the labels assigned to a node, use the LABELS function. It returns a collection of strings. Consider the following query:

```
MATCH (e {surname: "Davies"})
RETURN LABELS(e)
```

This query returns all the labels assigned to the nodes that have the surname property set to Davies. This function is useful when your database has nodes that have multiple labels.

# Working with paths and relationships

When you work with paths or with variable length relationships, you may need to inspect the relationships contained. The following functions are used for this purpose:

* TYPE
* ENDNODE and STARTNODE
* SHORTESTPATH and ALLSHORTESTPATHS
* RELATIONSHIPS

# TYPE

The string returned by this function is the type of the relationship passed. Consider the following query:

```
MATCH ()-[r]-()
RETURN TYPE(r), COUNT(*)
```

This query computes the number of relationships grouped by their type.

# ENDNODE and STARTNODE

The following functions inspect the nodes at the endpoints of a relationship:

- STARTNODE: This function returns the start node of the relationship passed as an argument

- ENDNODE: This function returns the end node of the relationship passed as an argument

These functions are useful when you haven't specified the direction of the relationship in the MATCH clause of a query, but you want all the related nodes and wish to know the direction of the relationship.

For example, in the HR management tool, the following query can be used:

```
MATCH (e:Employee {surname: "Davies"})-[r:REPORTS_TO]-(a:Employee)
RETURN a, ENDNODE(r)
```

This query looks for all the neighborhood nodes of the node with the surname property Davies (depth of one) along the relationship of REPORTS_TO. It returns the neighborhood and the employee who is at the end node of the relationship. In other words, it says who the boss is.

# SHORTESTPATH and ALLSHORTESTPATHS

The SHORTESTPATH and ALLSHORTESTPATHS functions search the shortest path among a set of paths. The difference is that while the SHORTESTPATH function returns at most one only path, the ALLSHORTESTPATHS function returns all the paths with the smallest depth in a collection of paths. Consider the following query:

```
MATCH p=SHORTESTPATH((a{surname:'Davies'})--(b{surname:'Doe'}))
RETURN p
```

The preceding query returns the shortest path between two employee nodes (Davies and Doe). Now, consider the following query:

```
MATCH p=SHORTESTPATH( (a {surname:'Davies'})--(b) )
RETURN p
ORDER BY LENGTH(p) DESC
LIMIT 1
```

Instead, the preceding query returns the path to the farthest node from a given employee node (Davies). In fact, once stated that the distance from a node is the shortest path from it, this query first computes all distances from all nodes, then selects the longest distance.

# RELATIONSHIPS

The RELATIONSHIPS function returns the collection of the relationships contained in a path. It is the equivalent of the NODES function. Consider the following query:

```
MATCH p = (a{surname:'Davies'})-[*..4]-(b{surname:'Taylor'})
RETURN RELATIONSHIPS(p)
```

This example takes all the paths with maximum depth of four between two nodes, then for each path, it returns the relationships visited.

# Working with collections

The following functions are used to manipulate or inspect a collection:

- HEAD
- TAIL
- LAST

## HEAD, TAIL, and LAST

The HEAD, TAIL, and LAST functions are used to work with collections as if they were lists. The HEAD function returns the first item of the collection, the TAIL function returns the rest of the list, while the LAST function returns the last item of the collection. Note that when you add the head of a collection to its tail (HEAD(c) + TAIL(c)), you get the full collection again.

If the collection is empty, the HEAD and the LAST functions will return a null value, while the TAIL function will return an empty collection. Consider the following query:

```
MATCH (a:Book)
RETURN HEAD(a.tags)
LIMIT 30
```

This query returns the first tag of the first 30 books found in the database.

# LENGTH

The LENGTH function returns the size of a collection of any type or of a string. Consider the following query:

```
MATCH (a:Book)
WHERE LENGTH(a.tags) >= 2
RETURN a
```

This example query returns all the books that have at least two tags. Note that the books without the tags property will be ignored because LENGTH(NULL) is a null value. Now, consider the following query:

```
MATCH (a:Book)
WHERE LENGTH(a.title) < 7
RETURN a
```

This example, instead, shows the function in action with a string. It returns all the books with a title shorter than seven characters in length.

# EXTRACT

The EXTRACT function is equivalent to the map function in the MapReduce paradigm. A similar function is included in most programming languages nowadays; for example, the map function in Scala, Java 8, JavaScript, and Ruby, the Select function in C#, and the list comprehensions in Python (although the map function is provided as well). It takes two parameters: a collection and an expression, which can be evaluated on each item of the collection. It returns a new collection, which has the values returned by the expression applied on every item of the collection. The syntax is similar to the syntax of the collection predicates (refer to *Chapter 2, Filter, Aggregate, and Combine Results*). Consider the following query:

```
RETURN EXTRACT(i IN [1,2,3] | i*2)
```

The result of this query is the collection `[2,4,6]` because it applies the expression `i*2` on every item `i` of the collection `[1,2,3]`. Now, consider the following query:

```
MATCH (a:Book)
RETURN EXTRACT(tag in a.tags | "Tag: " + tag)
LIMIT 30
```

For every book in the first 30 books found in the database, this query returns a list of strings with the prefix `Tag:`.

This function is mostly used with collections of nodes or relationships. Consider the following query:

```
MATCH p=(e:Employee {surname: "Davies"})-[r:REPORTS_TO*]
            -(a:Employee)
RETURN EXTRACT(node IN NODES(p) | LABELS(node))
```

The preceding query, for each node found in a path, extracts the labels of that node.

# FILTER

The `FILTER` function returns a collection created by adding values that satisfy a certain condition from a source collection. It is similar to the `WHERE` clause, but it works on collections. Consider the following query:

```
RETURN FILTER (x IN [1,2,3,4] WHERE x%2 = 0)
```

This simple query returns the even values from a list of integers. Yet, this query is mostly used while working with paths too. Now, consider the following query:

```
MATCH p=(e)-[r]->(a)
RETURN FILTER (node IN NODES(p) WHERE node:Book)
```

This query, for each path that matches the pattern, returns the list of nodes found in the path, but filters only the nodes with the label `Book`.

# REDUCE

The `REDUCE` function has the same purpose as the `Reduce` function of the well-known MapReduce paradigm. Nowadays, almost all languages have this function, even if sometimes with different names; the `reduce` function in Java 8 (the Stream API) and JavaScript, the `collect` function in Ruby and Python, the `Aggregate` function in C#, and the `foldLeft` function in Scala. It is used to aggregate the items of a collection, scanning every item and accumulating them according to a given expression. For example, the following query returns the sum of all items of a collection:

```
RETURN REDUCE (total = 0, i in [1,2,3] | total + i)
```

The variable `total` is the accumulator initialized to 0. Then for each item in the collection, this variable is increased by the value of the item. Of course, you can apply the same pattern to strings. Consider the following query:

```
RETURN REDUCE (text = "", i in ["Hello ","world","!"] | text + i)
```

This query concatenates the strings in the collections and returns `Hello world!`. Let's see a more realistic usage. Consider the following query:

```
MATCH p=(e:Book)-[r*]-(a)
WITH REDUCE (text = "",
        node IN NODES(p) |
            text + COALESCE(node.title, " * ") + "-") as TEXT
RETURN LEFT(text, LENGTH(text)-1)
```

This query, for each path found, returns a collection with the titles of the books found separated by a hyphen. In case a title is not found, thanks to the COALESCE function, an asterisk is returned instead of a `null` value. The last line of the query is needed to remove the last dash from the string.

# RANGE

The RANGE function is very simple; it returns a collection of integers contained in a numerical range, which is computed with the help of a given step. Consider the following query:

```
RETURN RANGE (1, 10, 2)
```

The preceding query returns `[1,3,5,7,9]`. The third parameter in the function is the step parameter, and is optional. By default, it is 1. Now, consider the following query:

```
RETURN RANGE (1, 5)
```

The preceding query returns `[1,2,3,4,5]` as the ranges are inclusive. Note that if you try to pass the step parameter as `0`, the query will fail with an error.

# Working with strings

Cypher provides a set of functions to work with strings. They are the typical string functions provided by most SQL databases. They are as follows:

- SUBSTRING, LEFT, and RIGHT
- STR
- REPLACE

- Trimming functions
- LOWER and UPPER

# SUBSTRING, LEFT, and RIGHT

The SUBSTRING, LEFT, and RIGHT functions are used when you want the substring of a given string. The following are their uses:

- SUBSTRING(source, index, length): This is a general function. It returns a string obtained by taking the characters of a given source string, from a given index, for a given length. If the length is not specified, it returns the string until the end.
- LEFT(source, length): This function returns a string of a given length, taking the first characters of the source string.
- RIGHT(source, length): This function returns a string of a given length, taking the last characters of the source string.

All of these functions will cause an exception if any index is negative, but won't cause any exception if the index is greater than the length of the string. In this case, they will just return an empty string.

The following query cuts the book where the titles are longer than four characters in length and append an ellipsis symbol at the end:

```
MATCH (a:Book)
RETURN LEFT(a.title, 4) + "..."
```

# STR

The STR function converts its unique argument to a string. It works on numbers, nodes, relationships, and paths. Consider the following query:

```
MATCH p=(a:Book{title:"Ficciones"})-[*]-()
RETURN STR(p)
```

This query returns the string representation of the path found with the MATCH clause. The result obtained is follows:

```
[Node[1027]{title:"Ficciones"},:AuthorOf[277]{},Node[1026]{name:"Jorge
Luis Borges"}]
```

 Conversion to integer values or to float values is not yet supported in Version 2.0.1, but two new functions (toInt and toFloat) were released along with the Version 2.0.2 to allow this conversion.

# REPLACE

The REPLACE function returns a string obtained by replacing all occurrences of a given string inside another string with a specified string. Consider the following query:

```
RETURN REPLACE("Cypher 1.9", "1.9", "2.0")
```

The preceding query will replace the occurrences of 1.9 in Cypher 1.9 with 2.0, returning Cypher 2.0. The REPLACE function can be used to remove all occurrences of a string as well. Consider the following query:

```
MATCH (a:Book)
RETURN REPLACE(a.title, "The ", "")
```

This query will return all the book titles after removing the The string.

## Trimming functions

Cypher provides three trimming functions. They are as follows:

- LTRIM: This function is used to remove whitespace characters from a given string from the left
- RTRIM: This function is used to trim a given string from the right
- TRIM: This function is used to trim a given string from both the left and the right

These three functions accept one string parameter and return the trimmed value. Consider the following query:

```
MATCH (a:Book)
RETURN TRIM(a.title)
```

The rows returned by this query are the book titles in the database without whitespaces at the beginning or at the end of the string.

## LOWER and UPPER

The LOWER function returns the lowercase version of a given string, while the UPPER function returns the uppercase version. They are often used to make a case-insensitive string comparison without using regular expressions. Consider the following query:

```
MATCH (a:Book)
WHERE UPPER(a.title) = UPPER("Learning Cypher")
RETURN a
```

The preceding query returns the book node that has the title Learning Cypher without caring for the case of the test string.

# Aggregation functions

We learned how to aggregate datasets and explored some aggregation functions in detail in *Chapter 2, Filter, Aggregate, and Combine Results*. Here, we summarize the aggregation functions and their usage. You can also find an extensive guide on the usage of groups and functions in this chapter.

## COUNT

The COUNT function is invoked with an argument, which can be an identifier or the * symbol. If this symbol is specified, the function will count all the rows in the dataset; otherwise, it will count the number of non-null values of the identifier. Consider the following query:

```
MATCH (aa: Person)
RETURN COUNT(a.surname)
```

This query returns the number of nodes with the label Person that have the property surname set. The COUNT function can be invoked with the DISTINCT clause to let it count only distinct values, as shown in the following query:

```
MATCH (a: Person)
RETURN COUNT(DISTINCT aa.surname)
```

## SUM

To sum the numerical values in a dataset, you can use the SUM function. Consider the following query:

```
MATCH (b:Book) <-[r:Votes]- (:User)
RETURN b, SUM(r.score)
```

This query returns the sum of the scores of the votes received by each book. The null values are ignored.

## AVG

The AVG function computes the average of a group of number values in the dataset. Consider the following query:

```
MATCH (b:Book) <-[r:Votes]- (:User)
RETURN b, AVG(r.score)
```

The rows returned by this query contain the average score of the votes received by a book. The null values are ignored in the computation of the average.

# PERCENTILEDISC and PERCENTILECONT

The PERCENTILEDISC and PERCENTILECONT functions compute the percentile of a value in a dataset. The difference between them is in the formula used. The PERCENTILEDISC function uses a discrete model for interpolation, while the PERCENTILECONT function uses a continuous model. A percentile measures the value below which a given percentage of items fall. Consider the following query:

```
MATCH (b:Book) <-[r:Votes]- (:User)
RETURN b, PERCENTILEDISC(r.score, 0.3)
```

This query returns, for each book, the thirtieth percentile of the score of votes for each book. It is a measure of the score below which 30 percent of the votes fall.

Note that there is no standard definition of percentile, but three possible definitions are available. An introduction to percentile definitions can be found at http://onlinestatbook.com/2/introduction/percentiles.html.

# STDEV and STDEVP

Standard deviation gives an estimate of the dispersion from the average. You should use the STDEVP function when you are computing the standard deviation for the whole population; otherwise, the STDEV function must be used. Consider the following query:

```
MATCH (b:Book) <-[r:Votes]- (:User)
RETURN STDEVP(r.score)
```

The return value of this query is the standard deviation of the score of the votes of all users.

A simple explanation of standard deviation can be found at http://www.mathplanet.com/education/algebra-2/quadratic-functions-and-inequalities/standard-deviation-and-normal-distribution.

# MIN and MAX

The MIN and MAX functions return the minimum and the maximum of a value in the dataset. Consider the following query:

```
MATCH (b:Book) <-[r:Votes]- (:User)
RETURN b, MIN(r.score), MAX(r.score)
```

The query returns all books voted by users, each with their minimum and maximum score received.

# Mathematical functions

Cypher provides a number of mathematical functions. Explaining all of them in detail is beyond the scope of this book. The following is a list of the most commonly used functions:

| Function | Return value |
|---|---|
| SIGN(x) | <ul><li>-1 if the given value is negative</li><li>0 if the given value is zero</li><li>1 if the given value is positive</li></ul> |
| ABS(x) | The absolute value of x |
| EXP(x) | The natural exponential function of x |
| LOG(x) | The natural logarithm of x |
| LOG10(x) | The common logarithm (base 10) of x |
| E() | The value of e (Euler's number), the base of natural logarithm |
| PI() | The value of pi |
| ROUND(x) | The value of x rounded to the nearest integer |
| RAND() | A random double value between zero and one |
| SQRT(x) | The square root of x |
| SIN(x) | The sine of x |
| COS(x) | The cosine of x |
| TAN(x) | The tangent of x |

# Index

community experience distilled

Thank you for buying

# Learning Cypher

## About Packt Publishing

Packt, pronounced 'packed', published its first book "*Mastering phpMyAdmin for Effective MySQL Management*" in April 2004 and subsequently continued to specialize in publishing highly focused books on specific technologies and solutions.

Our books and publications share the experiences of your fellow IT professionals in adapting and customizing today's systems, applications, and frameworks. Our solution based books give you the knowledge and power to customize the software and technologies you're using to get the job done. Packt books are more specific and less general than the IT books you have seen in the past. Our unique business model allows us to bring you more focused information, giving you more of what you need to know, and less of what you don't.

Packt is a modern, yet unique publishing company, which focuses on producing quality, cutting-edge books for communities of developers, administrators, and newbies alike. For more information, please visit our website: www.packtpub.com.

## About Packt Open Source

In 2010, Packt launched two new brands, Packt Open Source and Packt Enterprise, in order to continue its focus on specialization. This book is part of the Packt Open Source brand, home to books published on software built around Open Source licences, and offering information to anybody from advanced developers to budding web designers. The Open Source brand also runs Packt's Open Source Royalty Scheme, by which Packt gives a royalty to each Open Source project about whose software a book is sold.

## Writing for Packt

We welcome all inquiries from people who are interested in authoring. Book proposals should be sent to author@packtpub.com. If your book idea is still at an early stage and you would like to discuss it first before writing a formal book proposal, contact us; one of our commissioning editors will get in touch with you.

We're not just looking for published authors; if you have strong technical skills but no writing experience, our experienced editors can help you develop a writing career, or simply get some additional reward for your expertise.

Network Graph Analysis and
Visualization with Gephi

Visualize and analyze your data swiftly using dynamic network
graphs built with Gephi

Ken Cherven

# Network Graph Analysis and Visualization with Gephi

ISBN: 978-1-78328-013-1      Paperback: 116 pages

Visualize and analyze your data swiftly using dynamic network graphs built with Gephi

1. Use your own data to create network graphs displaying complex relationships between several types of data elements.

2. Learn about nodes and edges, and customize your graphs using size, color, and weight attributes.

3. Filter your graphs to focus on the key information you need to see and publish your network graphs to the Web.

Storm Real-time
Processing Cookbook

Efficiently process unbounded streams of data in real time

Quinton Anderson

# Storm Real-time Processing Cookbook

ISBN: 978-1-78216-442-5      Paperback: 254 pages

Efficiently process unbounded streams of data in real time

1. Learn the key concepts of processing data in real time with Storm.

2. Concepts ranging from Log stream processing to mastering data management with Storm.

3. Written in a Cookbook style, with plenty of practical recipes with well-explained code examples and relevant screenshots and diagrams.

Please check **www.PacktPub.com** for information on our titles

## OpenSceneGraph 3 Cookbook

ISBN: 978-1-84951-688-4        Paperback: 426 pages

Exactly 100 recipes to show advanced 3D programming techniques with the OpenSceneGraph API

1. Introduce the latest OpenSceneGraph features to create stunning graphics, as well as integration with other famous libraries.

2. Produce high-quality programs with short and familiar code.

3. Enriched with a lot of code and the necessary screenshots.

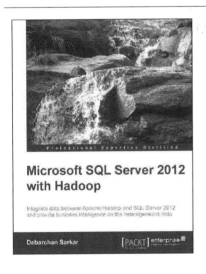

## Microsoft SQL Server 2012 with Hadoop

ISBN: 978-1-78217-798-2        Paperback: 96 pages

Integrate data between Apache Hadoop and SQL Server 2012 and provide business intelligence on the heterogeneous data

1. Integrate data from unstructured (Hadoop) and structured (SQL Server 2012) sources.

2. Configure and install connectors for a bi-directional transfer of data.

3. Full of illustrations, diagrams, and tips with clear, step-by-step instructions and practical examples.

Please check **www.PacktPub.com** for information on our titles

Made in the USA
Middletown, DE
28 October 2014